OLD PATHS
FOR
LITTLE FEET

Old Paths
for
Little Feet

Carol Brandt

Solid Ground Christian Books
Birmingham, Alabama

Solid Ground Christian Books
2090 Columbiana Rd., Suite 2000
Birmingham, AL 35216
205-443-0311
sgcb@charter.net
http://solid-ground-books.com

Old Paths for Little Feet
by Carol Brandt

Copyright 2003 by Carol Brandt
Tequesta, Florida
All Rights Reserved

All Scripture taken from *New Geneva Study Bible*
Copyright 1995 by Foundation for Reformation.

ISBN 1-932474-31-5

Manufactured in the United States of America

Carol Brandt has a B.A. in History from Florida State University and M.Ed. in Higher Education from Florida Atlantic University. She was nurtured in Southern Baptist churches. While teaching high school social studies, she incorporated thinking, writing, reading, and speaking skills into the curriculum. She has worked with Ernest C. Reisinger, a noted leader of the Founders Ministries to the Southern Baptist Convention, on several of his writings. She is married to John E. Brandt, O.D. and has two grown daughters.

*Dedicated to my mother,
Lottie Dickinson Cook*

Table of Contents

Preface 11

Promises to Remember 13

Introduction 15

Chapter 1
Love and Enjoy the Children 17

Chapter 2
Providence Dispels Fear 21

Chapter 3
The Providence of God is Sweet 25

Chapter 4
What We Believe Shapes Our Chatacter 29

Chapter 5
Grabbing at Straws 33

Chapter 6
Your Commitment Determines Your
Reaction to Resistance 37

Chapter 7
Children Need to See Your Fear of God 41

Chapter 8
Practical Hints for Instilling Reverence 45

Chapter 9
Check Your Grip 49

Chapter 10
Teach the Children that God is Their Creator 55

Chapter 11
Teach the Three Aspects of Sin 59

Chapter 12
Keep Your Balance 65

Chapter 13
Teach the Children the Ten Commandments 71

Chapter 14
Don't Give Your Child False Assurance 79

Chapter 15
Avoid Suspicion of Children's Faith 83

Chapter 16
Teach the Spiritual Disciplines 89

Chapter 17
Teach the Great Truths Plainly and Simply 95

Chapter 18
Keep Your Tools Handy 101

Conclusion 107

End Notes 109

Preface

Many good reasons could be given for publishing this book; I will give what I believe is the most important reason; the author has put her finger on that reason. It is that all Christian teaching, all Christian experience must have a sound doctrinal foundation. We live in a day when creeds, confessions and doctrinal instructions are almost lost in the religious circus of experience. Bishop Ryle said it well when he said that you can talk about religious experience all you wish but without doctrinal roots it will wither and die. Carol Brandt is showing the necessity of a doctrinal foundation in Christian experience. Biblical doctrine is more important than most parents, church members, preachers and teachers realize. Doctrine not only defines our beliefs, doctrine determines our direction and experience. Doctrine shapes our lives and our church programs. Doctrine is to the Christian what bones are to the body—I would not like a body without bones. Our author had this need in mind when she wrote this book. In my opinion, the doctrinal emphasis is the most important part of the book.

What doctrines am I talking about? I am talking about the doctrines of grace—those doctrines that were set forth, defined and defended at the Synod of Dort and later expressed in the Westminster Confession of Faith, the London Confession of 1689 and the Heidelberg Catechism. I am talking about those doctrines that set forth a sovereign God who actually saves sinners, not a little, impotent God who just makes salvation possible or just helps sinners to save themselves. I am talking about the doctrines that reveal the three great acts of the Triune God in recovering poor lost sinners. These three acts are election by the Father, redemption by the Son and calling by the Spirit. All these acts are directed to sinners, securing their salvation infallibly.

All that our author has written in this book is within this doctrinal framework. She writes for children to understand the doctrines of providence, depravity, regeneration, etc. The book crosses denominational lines and does not get bogged down on secondary issues. It furnishes many good examples on how to teach biblical doctrines such as providence, depravity, regeneration, assurance and the right use of the Ten Commandments to show the breach between the Creator and the creatures and furnishes us a fixed objective standard of righteousness for all creatures and for all times.

In summary, I suggest some reasons why parents, preachers, teachers and all who are interested in the souls of children should own and use *Old Paths for Little Feet:*

- It has a sound theological base.
- It is laced with Holy Scripture.
- It gives many helpful examples of how to teach Christian doctrine to children.
- It emphasizes teaching, teaching, teaching. This means no direct appeals to the will or the emotions, but rather a direct appeal to the mind and then appeal to the will and emotions. Our Lord was often addressed as, "Good Teacher."
- It contains many valuable quotes from such men as J. I. Packer, Dr. Martyn-Lloyd Jones, R. C. Sproul, Sinclair Ferguson, Dr. Tom Nettles.
- The author is an experienced teacher and an experienced mother. She makes the invisible, the eternal, and the infinite more understandable at a child's level.

Ernest C. Reisinger

Promises to Remember

"Thus says the Lord:
'Stand in the ways and see,
And ask for the *old paths,* where the good way is,
And walk in it;
Then you will find rest for your souls.'"
Jeremiah 6:16

"But the mercy of the Lord is from everlasting to everlasting
On those who fear Him,
And His righteousness to *children's children,*
To such as keep His covenant,
And to those who remember His commandments
to do them."
Psalm 103:17-18

"The secret things belong to the Lord our God,
but those things which are revealed belong to us
and to *our children* forever,
that we may do all the words of this law."
Deuteronomy 29:29

Introduction

"Stand in the ways and see,
And ask for the old paths, where the good way is,
And walk in it;
Then you will find rest for your souls."
Jeremiah 6:16

This book is written for mothers, grandmothers and ladies who aspire to be mothers and grandmothers one day. It is not another manual for raising children. It is not a system of child rearing techniques. There are plenty of those around.

Instead, this is a handbook for the rediscovery and passing on of biblical truths to the next generation. The "old paths" are applications of these truths. We need to dig up these worn paths, walk on them with our children and grandchildren, leading them to God and His grace. We need to educate ourselves in timeless truths and listen to voices from the past who have lived "where the good way is." So I have included some true stories of ladies from a variety of cultures and times who speak directly to us about their application of these principles.

> How to use this book

Signposts and resources are needed so that our busy lives don't rob our families of the direction and nurturing they require. Hopefully, this little book can function as both. Use it as a handbook; keep it handy for reference when a problem arises. You might read the whole book once just to give you an overview of family evangelism in historic Christianity. Each chapter teaches a biblical principle. Study that for yourself making sure you grasp the teaching and agree that it is a true principle of the scripture. Each chapter also contains an application of that principle to child rearing. When a question or problem arises in your family, use the Table of Contents to direct you to the area of need at the time. Read that chapter looking for the principle taught (the titles and ending bar are good clues). Think about the scriptures used. Listen to the voice from the past showing you one way another mother or grandmother applied those scriptures. Look at the End Notes for additional resources you can purchase to have on hand for your own understanding or to use with children. Why not talk it over with a friend who also wants to lead her children or grandchildren in spiritual things? You might use email if you're isolated from other women of like mind.

Not all of us have teaching skills. Our parenting and nurturing styles are different. God has not made us exactly alike; nor are our life experiences even remotely similar. We do not have to walk in lockstep or handle our children just like our neighbor or sister or mother! *But, each of us can discipline ourselves to keep on exercising faith, loving God and others, and changing how we live and think to please God (1 Timothy 2:15).* It takes self-control and perseverance to train children to look to Jesus Christ alone for their salvation and hope.

Let's train our children to walk on the old paths. Our reward will be rest for our own souls. And future generations will have clear hiking trails as they seek rest for their own souls.

Chapter 1

Love and Enjoy the Children

Lottie Moon, a Southern Baptist missionary to China, baked cookies to entice Chinese children to come and hear stories about Jesus. It was a way to get the children to listen to her. A little butter and sugar blended with some hugs and smiles—I'll bet they liked her, don't you?

> **PLAIN TEACAKE**
>
> 3 teacups of dry sugar
> 1 of butter
> 1 of sour milk
> 3 pints of flour
> 3 eggs, well beaten
> 1/2 teaspoon of soda
> Flavor to taste; roll thin and bake in a quick oven.
>
> Lottie Moon's Cookbook, 1872 [1]

In Psalm 34:11, children are told to come and listen so they can be taught the fear of the Lord, "*Come* you children, *listen* to me. I will teach you the fear of the Lord." Later, Jesus also said, "Let the little children *come* to Me."

"Come," not "Don't bother me." Lottie Moon wasn't saying "Get out of my kitchen." By her actions, she said, "Come!" David wanted to teach children to respect God and always remember He saw their every action and thought. So David said, "Come to me," not "Sit over there and listen to my experiences."

In his book, *Come Ye Children,* C. H. Spurgeon, a pastor in London in the mid 1800's, illustrates this principle with the following story:

"We have known some good men who are objects of abhorrence to children. You remember the story of two little boys who were one day asked if they would like to go to Heaven, and who, much to their teacher's astonishment, said that they really should not. When they were asked, 'Why not?' one of them said, 'I should not like to go to Heaven because Grandpa would be there, and he would be sure to say, 'Get along, boys; be off with you!' I should not like to be in Heaven with Grandpa.'" [2]

> "...If you drive a boy from you, your power over him is gone, for you will not be able to teach him anything."
>
> Charles Spurgeon

The idea of "Come" is an attitude as much as an embrace. Relish each developmental stage of childhood. Whether you're a teacher, a parent, or grandparent, enjoy, laugh over, and celebrate each quickly passing stage. By doing so, you are saying "Come."

A friend of mine is raising five children. One afternoon she was serving us tea on her deck while two kids played in a tent they'd made from sheets, another poured "tea" with us, and the baby crawled around. Suddenly the baby started lapping up rain puddles on the deck getting her face and clothes drenched—not to mention the possible germs. I probably would have jerked the baby up, grabbed the anti-bacterial soap, and huffed into cleaning up. My friend laughed in delight at the adorable wet baby and the confusion of the moment. She was relishing the "childish stages." You might disagree, choosing that incident to teach obedience or give a lesson on germs. But, delighting in childhood at some point communicates "Come" to children; you like them!

You also tell children you like them when you enjoy what they enjoy. Play is a wonderful thing. We used to have "play days" when we scheduled no other activities or work but planned a pirate's game or played in the pool. I have tried to welcome my neighbor's children into my kitchen. It is my way of saying,

"Come," and of getting them to like me. I let them help, stop everything and talk with them, or give them a healthy snack. The routine frequently includes reading a Bible verse or talking about God in some way.

One warning needs to be made: Never get the children to like you at the expense of condoning sin or forgetting who is in charge. Discipline gives stability and comfort to a child and sanity and survival to the adult! Christian principles are best received in a warm relational atmosphere balanced by clear boundaries and an underpinning knowledge of who is in charge. But, your children or grandchildren are not going to be taught to reverence God *by you* unless you have a welcoming attitude toward their childishness.

> *"What son is there whom a father does not chasten?"*
>
> Hebrews 12:7

Children won't hear us if they don't feel welcomed

Chapter 2

Providence Dispels Fear

Ann Judson, one of the first American missionaries, moved to Burma in 1813 with her husband, Adoniram. By 1826, she was dead at thirty-seven after much adversity. But her work helped found the Burmese church and preserve Adoniram's life for a further twenty-three years of mission work there. The publication of her *Memoir* in 1829 stirred a whole generation; she became a model of godly womanhood; she made a significant contribution to the missionary movement in the 1800's. She was courageous, steadfast, loyal, a teacher and defender of women and children.

The title of a new biography of Ann, *My Heart In His Hands,* by Sharon James, reveals Ann's reliance on God's providential care of His people. The secret of Ann's courage under great suffering is her application of the Bible's teaching on Providence:

Subjective experience (what she felt) was always based on objective reality (what she knew to be true, this knowledge being based on scripture). This was the reason for the strength and consistence of her spirituality.... The purpose of making this work accessible once again is so that this remarkable story may encourage Christians today to face whatever trials may confront them with the same confidence in the same God. [1]

Ann's trials included loneliness, illness, loss of children, lengthy separations from her husband, and the need to provide food for Adoniram while he was in an obscure prison. Ann increasingly relied on God's care:

> It is now six months since he left me, and not a single line has ever been received relative to the ship...I am trying to bear this state of uncertainty as a heavy affliction, a painful chastisement, from my heavenly Father, inflicted, no doubt, for wise and gracious purposes. [2] If I ever felt the value and efficacy of prayer, I did at this time. I could not rise from my couch; I could make no efforts to secure my husband; I could only plead with that great and powerful being who has said, **'Call upon me in the day of trouble and *I will hear*, and thou shalt glorify me'** and who made me at this time feel so powerfully this promise, that I became quite composed feeling assured my prayers would be answered. [3]

We can have that same confidence in an unchanging God...We can evaluate our feelings by the truth of scripture...We can apply the providence of God to our own situation...We can wonder at the uncertainties of life in general, yet trust in the faithfulness of God's promises. Hebrews 1:1-4 teaches that Jesus Christ was involved in creation and moves forward or upholds all things now, keeping creation safe from destruction.

> God,...has in these last days spoken to us by His Son, whom He has appointed heir of all things, through whom also He made the worlds, who being the brightness of His glory and the express image of His person, and upholding all things by the word of His power, when He had purged our sins, sat down at the right hand of

the Majesty on high, having become so much better than the angels, as He has by inheritance obtained a more excellent name than they.

The *New Geneva Study Bible* notes explain "upholding all things by the word of His power:"

> In the midst of history the Son's command holds the created order in existence (Col. 1:17; 2 Peter 3:4-7), preserving it from destruction until that day when His voice will remove all but the unshakable Kingdom of God and its heirs (12:26-28). [4]

God never changes. He has infinite power and wisdom. He uses that power wisely to hold the universe together so that everything can function as it was created to function. Even you. Even your kids!

My grandmother saw her two older sons off to Europe and the South Pacific during World War II. She told me of the agony she suffered at the thought of their being killed. Still trying to run the family farm after Edgar, her husband, died leaving one teen-aged son at home, her personal circumstances looked bleak. But her focus changed when she was vividly reminded that her heavenly Father had sacrificed His own Son for her. Who was she to complain? Like Ann Judson, her subjective feelings were evaluated in the light of scriptural truth, changing everything.

> *"I got up, wiped my tears and went back to work—a humbled, but more joyful mother."*
>
> Maude Caroline Dickinson

There is another aspect of the providence of God that is especially comforting to us. An old Baptist statement of faith puts it like this:

> As the providence of God doth in general reach to all creatures, so after a most special manner it taketh care of His church and disposeth of all things to the good thereof. [5]

The Baptist Faith and Message 2000 as adopted by the Southern Baptist Convention emphasizes the fatherhood of God in describing providence:

> God as Father reigns with providential care over His universe, His creatures, and the flow of the stream of human history according to the purposes of His grace. He is all powerful, all loving, and all wise. [6]

God's care reaches to everything He has made. And isn't it logical that He would have a special concern for His own children? The biblical account of Esther gloriously illustrates this truth. It took place in the Persian Empire, centered in today's Iran and Iraq and stretching from India to Ethiopia about 470 B.C. God used Queen Esther to influence the Emperor to favor the Jews and execute their enemy, Haman. It is a real incident, not a "story."

God's providence should be in your heart and on your mind. You should teach it to your children and talk to them of Esther and Ann Judson. You should tell of your own experiences affirming God's providential care of you and those of your family, friends, and even people from history. It should impact your actions and how you see life. Even though a lot of what happens can't be explained, reasoned, or the "whys" answered now, the clear teaching of scripture is that God does micromanage for the favor of His people. It frees you to love and enjoy by putting your fears in perspective.

Understanding God's providence while relying on His grace gives you courage to face whatever troubles come your way.

CHAPTER 3

The Providence of God is Sweet

The providence of God is that sweetness that makes some of the harder biblical teachings palatable. To train a child to go the way he should, we need to "touch his palate" so he has a taste for the sweet things of God (Proverbs 22:6). One way to give this "sugar" is to tell stories. Children who love us will listen to stories that illustrate God's care, upholding, and governing of individuals, groups, nations, and animals. And telling stories is another wonderful way to say "Come."

I immediately think of King David's life—events dramatically illustrating God's special care over him. He was rescued from being torn apart by a lion and a bear. He defeated the giant, making him a national hero. He was protected from Saul's attempts to kill him. He became king. He experienced God's forgiveness and reconciliation even after ordering the sure death of another man to cover up an illicit love affair. You can make these into exciting stories that teach life lessons and tantalize the child's interest in whether God might favor him in that same way. And you can take the child to the Psalm songs of deliverance time after time. Or sing those songs of deliverance together. (See Psalms 107-118 especially.)

Another intriguing example of this plain and simple truth of God's care and ordering of all things for the good of His people is David's marriage to the recently widowed Abigail. Abigail's husband was mean and hateful and a drunk. Abigail tried to cover for him when he openly opposed David whom she knew was God's man (1 Samuel 25). Suddenly her husband died! She marries David (and brings with her all her wealth)! Don't forget to stress that there is no evidence in the scriptures of any sexual impurity or lust between Abigail and David. Today's media writers would never write it that way!

You could tell these stories beginning and ending with a brief summary statement of the providential teaching. For instance, "You know that God made you and all things, don't you? Well, He takes care of you and all things too. Look how He took care of_____ when_____. Then discuss how it spotlights God's goodness, His wisdom, power, mercy, etc. Our children deserve more than just cute stories. But, storytelling is a super way to illustrate biblical themes.

Children love to hear stories about people they know too—aunts, uncles, parents, cousins, etc.—back in the "olden" days. Be sure to spell out how God was glorified through the event.

When I was in elementary school, we lived in Homestead, Florida, where we had some chickens and several cats. My brother, Ed, decided to bathe all the cats. Their bath didn't include a toweling down, so they looked like scarecrows scowling on the front porch. To my mother's horror, the pastor and his wife chose that moment to drop by for a pastoral visit. Stringy-looking cats were everywhere. It turned out that Mrs. Whit had a phobia of cats; she wouldn't get out of the car. After kindly making his apologies, Dr. Whit backed out of the driveway. Ed was in trouble! My brother and I laughed and laughed, but I remembered how kind Dr. Whit was to his wife and my embarrassed mother. I liked him, and warmly welcomed him when he returned to see if I understood the gospel. God used my brother's prank to show me Dr. Whit's kindness. So I listened to him when he came to the Christmas party for my Sunday School class, and when he later returned to our home to go over the gospel. Dr. Whit's kindness drew me to the Savior. This could be my story to illustrate God's providential care of me. What is your story? Tell it to children.

Be sure to distinguish between the truth of the scriptures, life stories, and our interpretation of our own stories. Some postmodernists in liberal Christian circles teach that all stories are equally "truth," so we can tell ours and listen to others, but there really isn't any truth. They sensitively listen to others and tell their own stories, but Bible stories are "stories," not truth to them. Many United Methodists, United Presbyterians, some Southern Baptists and others have departed from historic Christianity and their denomination's heritage in this way. We should make sure our children understand that our interpretation of events could be fallible; only God's word is truth. It is also important to be truthful to children about the unanswered questions of life. Some things that happen are a mystery for now.

Leading Little Ones to God by Marian Schoolland teaches providence by using the visual word picture of a shepherd. Here is an example of her use of this simple image:

> Yes, all God's people are Jesus' sheep. Boys and girls are Jesus' lambs. He loves them. He watches over them, just as David watched over the lambs in his flock. God loves us. He takes care of us. [1]

She then reads *Psalm* 23 and has the children sing "Savior, Like a Shepherd Lead Us." Psalm 23 is full of word pictures that comfort us as we visualize them. Your children need that visual comfort too. Draw pictures with words. Those images will stay on the mind a long time and return often.

Tell of the wonders of God's Providence as you "go in and out."

CHAPTER 4

What We Believe Shapes Our Character

Suzannah Spurgeon fell in love with her pastor. Imagine that dilemma! In the 1850's when Queen Victoria ruled the British Empire, Charles H. Spurgeon's preaching took London by storm. Her pastor gave Suzannah a copy of *The Pilgrim's Progress*. A few years before her death, Mrs. Spurgeon wrote about their ensuing romance:

> God Himself united our hearts in indissoluble bonds of true affection, and, though we knew it not, gave us to each other forever. [1]

Trials and suffering inevitably came. Pressures increased because of Spurgeon's doctrinal beliefs and because of their own physical pains:

> I deemed it my joy and privilege to be ever at his side, accompanying him on many of his preaching journeys, nursing him in his occasional illnesses,—...I mention this, not to suggest any sort of merit on my part, but simply that I may here record my heartfelt gratitude to God, that, for a period of ten blessed years, I was permitted to encircle him with all the comforting care and tender affection which it was in a wife's

"Afterwards, God ordered it otherwise."
Suzie Spurgeon

power to bestow. Afterwards, God ordered it otherwise. He saw fit to reverse our position to each other; and for a long, long season, suffering instead of service became my daily portion, and the care of comforting a sick wife fell upon my beloved. [2]

Mrs. Spurgeon is expressing a reliance on God's power and right to carry out what He deems is good for each of His children. That over-riding power is His sovereignty—another awesome concept to whet your child's tastebuds for the things of God. Dab a bit of sovereignty on those tastebuds and blend in a dab of providence. Susie Spurgeon shows us how to teach it while telling our own experience. Susie believed that God gave them to each other, knit their hearts together in love and allowed her to "serve" her husband for ten wonderful years. Then her health problems began. Both were from God—to be accepted from a loving father who had her good in mind.

What we teach our children about God will shape what they believe. Their own beliefs about God will shape their character. In an article on "The Challenge of the Third Millennium," J. I. Packer says:

> Children are growing up without any knowledge of the Bible or its morality. Sometimes they are taught only the gospel and not the law. They are not being raised in stable, nurturing families. As a result, the middle-aged adults of the next century will have grown bodies but stunted characters. They will be quite infantile in their emotional lives and incapable of steady commitments. [3]

Ann Judson, converted during the Second Great Awakening in New England in 1806, had "an overwhelming awareness of the majesty of God and her own unworthiness." [4] Her doctrine of God included an emphasis on the sovereignty of God and the contrasting sinfulness of man that sustained her during great hardships in Burma.

Ann and Adoniram had no sense of God "needing" them; in a real sense they believed that what happened to them was of secondary importance. A sovereign God could use them as long as He wanted but then raise up others in their place. Their religion was God-centered, not man-centered. [5]

One of my Florida friends, Leilou, has been an encouragement to me with her light-heart resulting from a practical reliance on the sovereignty of God. With so many trendy churches to choose from, a young girl asked Lei which to attend. The response came in a gentle, southern way: "Dear, I have found that I need to regularly be reminded of God's goodness and control so I look for a church that teaches both." Is this her secret to a warm, positive outlook on life?

> *"I need to regularly be reminded of God's goodness and control."*
>
> Leilou Brady

J.I. Packer relates all this to what he calls "growing downwards:"

> We should focus on our relationship with God in light of His greatness, holiness, and awesomeness. If we'd appreciate these qualities more we'd be a humbler lot of people than we are. And our hearts and consciences would be more sensitive to God's glory. [6]

Follow Susie and Ann's examples. Focus on God's sovereignty and providential care. Then talk about it with the children as you go about your daily life. It will whet their appetites for the things of God.

What we teach our children about God will affect their character development.

Chapter 5

Grabbing At Straws

I taught high school history, government, and economics. As a twenty-two year old graduate of Florida State University with no teaching experience and little supervised training in education, I was hired to teach comparative government to one hundred seniors. The catch was that there was no textbook for the course; no approved body of knowledge all drawn up and attractively packaged for me to dispense! Taking it a day at a time, I planned my lessons the night before and made quick changes on lesson plans while I drove to work. A lot depended on what was on the news that day! It didn't work; I was soon in trouble.

> *"I made quick changes the night before. I was grabbing at straws."*
>
> Carol Cook

You will be in big trouble too if you take this approach to training your children in the nurture and admonition of the Lord. It took me several years of teaching to develop a systematic body of knowledge from which to teach comparative government and economic systems. When you're responding to the immediate needs of children, it's a little difficult to put together the whole teaching of the Bible in a form that can be transferred from one generation to another!! You'll be grabbing at straws like I was. And you have much more at stake here than I did.

These are your own children and grandchildren we're talking about!

Happily, we are not left in this position. Confessions of Faith are statements of what the adherents believe the Bible teaches. Denominations and individual churches usually have such a document. The Apostles' Creed and the Nicene Creed were two of the earliest attempts to systematic biblical interpretation. The Anglicans in England had their Articles of Faith from the early 1600's. The *Westminster Confession of Faith* with its larger and shorter catechisms, written 1643-49, sought this same objective for Presbyterians. Baptists in colonial America chose to organize themselves around confessions of faith both within local churches and their associations.[1] *The Baptist Confession of Faith of 1689* was republished by Charles Spurgeon in the 1860's because,

> We need a banner because of the truth; it may be that this small volume may aid the cause of the glorious gospel by testifying plainly what are its leading doctrines. [2]

It was already known in America as *The* Baptist Confession. The *Savoy Catechism of 1658* also attempted these same objectives of systematic presentation and raising a banner of truth for Congregationalists.

"Who cares about all this? I just want to get on with leading my children to love God. Let the church leadership worry about keeping the church teachings right and raising banners!" Is that your objection?

In his study of catechisms in Baptist life, *Teaching Truth, Training Hearts,* Tom Nettles asserts that catechisms can be both a hedge and a wedge. They can hedge in the truth and also wedge open the mind to think on the great doctrines, and hopefully, start young minds asking questions. Catechisms and confessions of faith are tools we can use in the rediscovery of truths believed through the years by other Christians. I used *A Catechism For Boys and Girls* with my girls, and even though my efforts were haphazard and less demanding than they could have been, the simple questions kept us on track and made me (and I hope the children) think on great ideas. (As an aside, it certainly added an element of "spice" to homemaking since I could think about these truths while I cleaned, cut grass, or supervised children.) My mother didn't know about catechisms and most of my church leaders "shot from the hip," so to speak, rather than organizing their beliefs around confessions or catechisms. So catechizing was new to our family and friends.

"But isn't having a Bible without error enough?" someone might object. My former pastor, Ernest Reisinger writes:

> It is important to have an inerrant Bible, but what good is an inerrant Bible if we do not know what it teaches or how to apply it to every day practice? Many heretics and cults believe the *Bible*. However, it is their interpretation as to what the *Bible* teaches that has led them to their cultic and heretical views. This is why the Creeds and Confessions came into existence. The Creeds and Confessions were born out of controversy as to what the *Bible* teaches. [3]

> "What good is an inerrant Bible if we do not know what it teaches...?"
> Ernest Reisinger

The ladies from history we've mentioned, Suzie Spurgeon, Ann Judson, and my friend, Leilou Brady, have all had access to basically the same confession of faith and have adhered to it. The confession helped them know what the Bible means. It helped me to interpret Abigail's story as well. It will help you whet the children's appetites for knowing God and living authentic lives.

Remember my senior government class and the troubles I brought on myself with spur of the moment lesson plans? The value of examining a confession of faith, and adapting it for your own, is that it becomes a handy reference source for teaching your children. Most include scripture footnotes, the words are carefully chosen, the topics clearly set forth. Voila! Your lesson plan! You can quickly find the verses needed to teach that God is wise; that He works out all things for our good; that we reap what we sow; that sin has consequences.

Confessions of faith and catechisms, *rightly used,* can aid us greatly in leading our children to love and serve God. Can't you hear these questions: "Is the Holy Spirit the third God?" "My teacher says that the universe began with a big bang." "How can I be saved?"

Let's be sure we believe our confession of faith and then use it to teach children what the Bible says, what it means, and how they can apply it. Where is your confession of faith? A tool is only useful if you can find it!

> *Confessions of faith help us instruct our children*

Chapter 6

Your Commitment Determines Your Reaction to Resistance

Deuteronomy 6, given by God through Moses to His people in the mid-second millennium B.C., can be applied to us today. Those who have trusted in Jesus Christ are God's chosen people. Christians today are like the nation of Israel who were Abraham's descendants through Issac, the promised child: "If you are Christ's, then you are Abraham's seed and heirs according to the promise" (Galatians 3:29).

These Galatians' verses are like bifocals in our glasses through which we can see (and understand) the Old Testament teachings. Now with your "gospel spectacles" on, go back to Deuteronomy 7:6-13; 10:12-22; 11:18-21. Seeing this through the teachings of Galatians enables us to apply these promises to ourselves since we are "children of the promise" as well.

We are God's special treasure. He loves us and keeps His promises of mercy to us while He condemns those who hate Him.

> "Therefore, you shall lay up these words of mine in your heart and in your soul, and bind them as a sign on your head, and they shall be as frontlets between your eyes. You shall teach them to your children, speaking of them when you sit in your house, when you walk by the way, when you lie down, and when you rise up. And you

shall write them on the doorposts of your house and on your gates, that your days and the days of your children may be multiplied in the land of which the Lord swore to your fathers to give them, like the days of the heavens above the earth" (Deut. 11:18-21).

Read these verses out loud; rejoice in their comfort; think about your responsibilities.

When my two daughters were in their teens, John and I ran into a little resistance to our morning prayer and brief application of a scripture. There was much more pressure on the girls from their peers to have beautiful hair and trendy clothes than to develop godly characters. They hated breakfast; John was in a hurry too; the phone was already ringing. But, we wanted to apply these Deuteronomy passages. My former pastor (who was always sending me books) sent me *Signposts From Proverbs* which arranges the teachings according to topics like money, lying, gossip, self-control, etc.[1] This little book served as our "doorposts" and "gates" to the family's going in and out to daily activities in Indiana. John and I prayed together (sometimes the girls would join us); a proverb was read aloud as each person grabbed (or avoided!) their breakfast, heading out the door. We tried to discuss its meaning or application to a specific attitude or relationship. Teens like proverbs because they are short and practical. Sometimes we did the same proverb for a week or several proverbs on the same topic. But, each was wrapped in prayer and we felt this partially fulfilled our commitment to make our household aware of God's teachings.

> *"Better a little with the fear of the Lord than great wealth with turmoil."*[2] Proverbs 15:6

How would you rate your commitment to raise your children in the nurture and admonition of the Lord?

In his book, *I Want To Enjoy My Children*, Dr. Henry Brandt, a Christian psychologist, asserts:

In our experience, however, parents speak of the maintenance of the family devotion as a difficult task. The children sometimes resist it. It is difficult to keep interesting. Parents are forever looking for some book or other aid that would make it more attractive. The success of the family devotions, in our opinion, is a matter of conviction more that a matter of technique or carefully chosen material. The basic question is: Is it vital to the welfare of your child?...As you consider the family devotions vital to the child's and your welfare, you will see that it is carried out. You will overlook resistance to it as you do in other matters. [2]

> *"You will overlook resistance to it as you do to other matters."*
>
> Dr. Henry Brandt

Commitment works itself out in varying ways depending upon our circumstances. Mary C. Lee, General Robert E. Lee's wife, wrote to her daughter in the years after America's War Between the States:

> I am glad to hear my darling little Rob is becoming so sweet and good. Don't spoil him. I fear he will have too many indulgences to make a great and self-controlled spirit essential to a great and good man; but we must pray that God will direct him in all his ways and teach him early to love and serve Him. Kiss him for his Gran, who is now looking forward to seeing him next summer, when he will no doubt be able to ride Lucy, with Fritz behind and Love before. (Lucy was their horse, Fritz and Love were cats. Rob was three.) [3]

Mrs. Lee couldn't be with her grandchild regularly so she stayed involved through correspondence with her daughter-in-law, prayer, and looking forward to a summer visit. But commitment was there.

Resistance can also take varying forms. Sometimes it's not so childish. Monica, the mother of Augustine, lived long before Mary and Robert E. Lee. She ran into hard resistance to her efforts to raise a godly boy in North Africa in the 4th century A.D. Her husband didn't help her or set a good example. Her hope and prayers were for her son's salvation. But, Augustine rebelled and lived a wayward life until age 33. He resisted her teaching and life example. Finally, upon seeing the reality of his conversion, she told him:

> Son, for my own part I have no further delight in anything in this life. What I do here any longer, and to what end I am here, I know not, now that my hopes in this world are accomplished. One thing there was for which I desired to linger for a while in this life, that I might see you a Christian before I died... [4]

Monica was dead in two weeks. Augustine went on to become an esteemed church leader and champion for truth not only to his generation but down through the ages. Her commitment to her task outlasted the resistance.

What kind of resistance are you facing? Listen to these voices from the past, role models from widely different times, cultures, and circumstances, who faced resistance and persevered.

If you are not committed to instructing your children, their natural resistance will gain control and you will let it slip (or hope someone else is doing it!). Expect resistance. They are children after all.

> *The degree of our commitment to family evangelism will determine how we handle resistance or manipulation.*

CHAPTER 7

Children Need to See Your Fear of God

Now that you have all the answers about God's sovereignty and providence, we can look at how these doctrines relate to life and character. (Of course, I'm joking. It took me years to iron out my natural objections to these interpretations; swayed by Protestant church history, Deuteronomy 29:29, and a winsome attractiveness in the lives of other adherents, I finally laid aside my objections.) You may have already raised some objections of your own, particularly to the parts of sovereignty we haven't studied. But, I urge you to lay aside your emotions for the moment as we focus on the impact a sincere holding to these doctrines has on our character. As we have seen, belief in sovereignty and providence lead to a magnification of God's majesty, power, mercy, and grace. When these traits are emphasized and contrasted with our human weaknesses, we are humbled to stand in awe of God. Then we are standing on one of the "old paths."

> "In a world where people are increasingly hopeless, Gospel ministers must present Christ and the new life in Him as the only beacon of light in a very dark cultural situation."
>
> J.I. Packer

J.I. Packer has predicted that the observable desperate condition in our culture today will lead to feelings of despair and hopelessness in the years to come. Dr. Packer believes the

41

only solution for America is a return to "the Puritan understanding of God—great in judgment as He is great in grace."[1] Our man-centeredness must decrease in our daily lives and in our worship, while we grow in the knowledge and adoration of God.

Look at the character traits found in the following verses:

> The fear of the Lord is the beginning of wisdom,
> And the knowledge of the Holy One is understanding.
> Proverbs: 9:10

> In the fear of the Lord there is a strong confidence,
> And his children will have a place of refuge.
> The fear of the Lord is a fountain of life,
> To turn one away from the snares of death.
> Proverbs 14:26-27

> Happy is the man who is always reverent,
> But he who hardens his heart will fall into calamity.
> Proverbs 28:14

> Charm is deceitful and beauty is passing,
> But a woman who fears the Lord, she shall be praised.
> Proverbs 31:30

Fear of God is defined as a "reverential fear," a wholesome dread of displeasing Him, not a terror that tries to get out of His presence.[2] Adam and Eve became more interested in hiding from God than in seeking to please Him. Their fear turned to terror. Jacob referred to his father's God as "Fear" (Genesis 31:42). Issac must have modeled reverence for God before his family. It "came back" to the adult Jacob. (The same thing happened to John Newton in the 1770's "when he remembered" his mother's reverence for God. He later wrote "Amazing Grace.") This "wholesome dread of displeasing God" is mingled with love and wonder. It is love for a suffering Savior, and wonder that God's plan and initiative could include "even me." Fear like this is wise. It leads to confidence and praise and erupts into true life.

Jesus teaches about this wholesome dread of displeasing a God who ultimately will hold us accountable in Luke 12. In warning against a spreading hypocrisy, He ties together ultimate judgment with the love that only God can give. He reminds us that we'd better dread displeasing God, "For there is nothing covered that will not be revealed, nor hidden that will not be known. Therefore whatever you have spoken in the dark will be heard in the light, and what you have spoken in the ear in inner rooms will be proclaimed on housetops" (Luke 12:2-3).

Fear like this is wise. It is an old path that leads to confidence and praise and erupts into true life. Fear but don't fear. Be in awe but don't shrink away in terror, cowardice, or timidity, because of the wonderful love of God.

> "Though the fig tree may not blossom,...And the fields yield no food;...Yet, I will rejoice in the Lord, I will joy in the God of my salvation."
>
> Habakkuk 3:17-18

In our post-modern culture of relativity and constant redefinition of truth, rein yourself in and conduct a hypocrisy check:

Are you standing on the old path that exhibits a reverence for God and a wholesome fear of His judgment? Or do you claim to believe in a Judgment Day yet look at God as your "buddy" who overlooks your shortcomings? Have you over-emphasized God's love? Are you more conscious of what others think or of pleasing God? Are you missing the joy and comfort of knowing that you are of great value to the Creator who watches over even the smallest birds? Are you gradually "growing downwards," falling to your knees before a God who will one day hold each of us accountable?

Your children, like Jacob, are watching. They will remember.

> *A balanced focus on God's sovereignty and majesty will humble us and give us hope.*

CHAPTER 8

Practical Hints for Instilling Reverence

We can't instill reverence and fear of God into our children if we have none in ourselves. That is our starting point in this process. Youngsters can smell a hypocrite! That's the reason for your hypocrisy check in Chapter Seven.

King Ahab was under Jezebel's thumb: her influence gave official support in Israel to the worship of Baal. Ahab even built a temple for Baal in Samaria during the time when Elijah was God's spokesman. Talk about a dark and desperate culture! Yet Ahab enjoyed the service of a godly man right under his wife's nose. Obadiah was probably in charge of administering the palace and overseeing the King's properties.[1] His name means "servant of Jehovah." Think about this godly businessman's tensions. The historical account unfolds in 1 Kings 18.

It is an encouragement to picture Obadiah managing Ahab's property. (Perhaps God has a believing man or woman serving at the right hand of your President, Governor or Mayor.) Then he risked his life by hiding and feeding one hundred prophets during Jezebel's massacre. He feared God, not Baal. Obadiah was cautious and prudent. Yet, he believed Elijah, and so used his relationship with King Ahab to arrange a showdown which resulted in the execution of 850 prophets of Baal and Asherah (1 Kings 18:19; 40).

Ahab and his father ruled Israel for thirty-four years during a downhill slide of cultural immorality and idolatry. Can you relate to the task of Obadiah's parents as you seek to raise children who love God today? Finding the "old paths" can take a lot of work.

> *"For the grace of God to convert a man like Paul, who is full of threatenings against the saints, is a great marvel; but for the grace of God to preserve a believer for ten, twenty, thirty, forty, fifty years, is quite as great a miracle and deserves more of our praise than it usually commands."*
>
> Charles Spurgeon

Obadiah hints at how he was raised: "But I your servant have feared the Lord from my youth" (1 Kings 18:12). We aren't privy to any details. But Obadiah's parents must have been willing to take risks. They certainly took one in choosing his name. They could have blended into their culture better with another choice. So they must have found this path of reverence and awe toward God before he was born.[3] Obadiah's parents must have desired to raise a godly son or they wouldn't have chosen this name.

You need to desire that your children will seek after God while still children, growing in wise living and reverence toward God as they increase in physical strength. It should be a desire of your heart while you are delighting in God yourself. "Delight yourself also in the Lord, And He shall give you the desires of your heart" Psalm 37:4.

The following are some ways you might instill right fear of God in your children:

- Tell them about the coming Judgment Day and Hell. Don't make light of either or skirt the subjects. Mention them when someone dies to expose the reality of a God who can (and does) condemn. One of our "voices from the past," Frances Havergal, included these frightful topics in her bedtime stories so the children would think on serious topics once the candles were out.

- Always teach together the two truths about God's love and mercy contrasted with His judgment. Join both truths like your hands join together for an effective golf grip. The two gripped together are strong. Don't teach the one without teaching the other.
- Avoid casualness about God: i.e. "God is my co-pilot;" "The Man Upstairs." In our Bible School recently, the songs and body motions we taught really bothered me. I felt like a cheerleader at a pep rally. And this was done during the worship assembly! "Am I just getting too old for this?" I asked. But, the real issue was the casual attitude toward God that was communicated. This was not one of the "old paths." We need to rediscover the majesty of God that was taught to generations of children.
- Pick your pastor carefully. What the children hear from the pulpit really matters! Does he make light of God? Does he join the truths, keeping his teaching balanced?
- What are they hearing in "children's church"? Is it like the Bible school I saw? You should know. Or maybe it would be better to keep them with you, hearing what you hear, talking about it later.
- Participate in family and corporate worship that is reverent. Avoid casual, light, entertaining services. The same goes for children's worship. Think about what the order of service and music are teaching about God. Keep them with you if you pick up on light and entertaining to the neglect of reverent and majestic.
- Train your children to honor their parents and other rightful authorities. How will they grow in their

reverence for God if they don't learn to honor you?
- ❋ Don't be a hypocrite. Reverence God. Dread displeasing Him.

> *Casualness about God robs us and our children of true praise and humility.*

Chapter 9

Check Your Grip

We've used the golf grip as a picture of entwining the truths of scripture. The golf grip is strengthened by encircling a finger from each hand. This causes the two hands to act as one. Try it and you'll see what I mean. Failing to entwine the fingers results in two hands working separately, often fighting against one another. That makes it more difficult to keep the ball going straight and get the distance you need.

> *"I do hold that there is no doctrine of the Word of God which a child, if he be capable of salvation, is not capable of receiving. I would have children taught all the great doctrines of truth without a solitary exception, that they may in their after day hold fast by them."*
>
> Charles Spurgeon

Teaching biblical principles is like that too. The doctrinal truths need to be entwined for strength and distance. Visualize the love of the Father for His children as the left hand while the right hand is judgment by the sovereign God. Teach one; teach the other. Your children will be strengthened to go the distance. But, if you teach only the love of the Father, what do you think will happen to reverence and awe of a majestic God? Or if you talk only of God's judgment, what will happen to warm little hearts who want to trust the Father? Direct their little feet to the old paths.

No one can tell you exactly when or how to teach these to your child. Charles Spurgeon maintained that, "As soon as children can learn evil, be assured that they are competent, under the teaching of the Holy Spirit, to learn good."[2] It is all in how the truths are presented and joined together. Sensitivity to child development and awareness of children's powers of imagination should be your guides as to the how and when.

Death and the last judgment are concisely presented in the *Westminster Confession of Faith*[3] and *The Baptist Confession of 1689*[4] and *The Baptist Faith and Message 2000*. They teach the following interpretations of scriptures which can serve as a handy guide for instruction or a quick reference when questions pop up:

1. After death our souls live on. Believers go to Christ; unbelievers to hell and torment. (2 Cor. 5:1-8, Luke 6:23-24, 1 Peter 3:19).
2. At the last day, all souls will be united forever to their own bodies either to honor or dishonor. The godly who are still alive will be changed. (1 Cor. 15:42-44, 1 Cor. 15: 51-52).
3. There will be a specific judgment day when each person must give an account to Christ and either be rewarded or punished. (2 Cor. 5:10, Rom. 14:10-12, Matt. 12:36-37).
4. God's mercy and justice will be made known through this judgment. The righteous will inherit everlasting life and fullness of joy; those who do not know God through Christ will be relegated to everlasting torments and denied the presence of the Lord. (2 Thess. 1:7-10, Matt. 25:21, 34, 46).
5. We are to believe in this day coming so that all men will be deterred from sin and so that the godly will be comforted in their adversity as they wait for rewards. The exact day is kept secret so that we may watch and look for it (Matt. 25:21, Matt. 24:36-44, 2 Thess. 1:5-7).

We have another voice from the past helping us to stay balanced. Anne Cousin read the letters of Samuel Rutherford from the 1600's in Scotland. She lived 1824-1906 but they still spoke to her. She wrote a hymn in 1857 based on his letters and his last words. Listen to the balance:

>The sands of time are sinking,
>   The dawn of heaven breaks,
>The summer morn I've sighed for,
>   The fair sweet morn awakes;
>Dark, dark hath been the midnight,
>   But dayspring is at hand,
>And glory, glory dwelleth
>   In Emmanuel's land.
>
>The King there in his beauty
>   Without a veil is seen;
>It were a well-spent journey
>   Though sev'n deaths lay between:
>The Lamb with his fair army
>   Doth on Mount Zion stand,
>And glory, glory dwelleth
>   In Emmanuel's land.
>
>O Christ, he is the fountain,
>   The deep sweet well of love!
>The streams on earth I've tasted
>   More deep I'll drink above:
>There to an ocean fulness
>   His mercy doth expand,
>And glory, glory dwelleth
>   In Emmanuel's land.
>
>With mercy and with judgment
>   My web of time He wove,
>And aye the dews of sorrow
>   Were lustred with His love:

> I'll bless the hand that guided,
>   I'll bless the heart that plann'd,
> When thron'd where glory dwelleth
>   In Immanuel's land.
>
> Oh! I am by Beloved's
>   And my Beloved's mine!
> He brings a poor vile sinner
>   Into His "house of wine."
> I stand upon His merit,
>   I know no other stand,
> Not e'en where glory dwelleth
>   In Immanuel's Land!
>
> The bride eyes not her garment,
>   But her dear bride-groom's face;
> I will not gaze at glory,
>   But on my King of grace;
> Not at the crown he giveth,
>   But on his pierced hand;
> The Lamb is all the glory
>   Of Emmanuel's land. [5]

Anne Ross Cousin had dug up the old worn path traveled by Samuel Rutherford two hundred years before. There it is stretching before us...

> *"God hath appointed a day, wherein He will judge in righteousness, by Jesus Christ,...all persons that have lived upon earth shall appear before the tribunal of Christ, to give an account of their thoughts, words, and deeds."*
> The Westminster Confession of Faith

It is wrong to deny children the warnings and blessings inherent in this teaching. They need to glimpse God's mercy —

and, concurrently, flee His wrath and it consequences. I have a dear friend who somehow never grasped that God would hold believers accountable for their stewardship of His blessings. Her grip was weakened because she emphasized the mercy of God but omitted the accountability of a believer with the possibility of losing rewards.

I hope this helps strengthen your grip on what the Bible says about judgment and mercy. You can see how its anticipation can lead to an awe of God's justice and a love of His mercy. Right application of it can deter us from sinning, and encourage us when our service to God is difficult. It is an "old path;" we need to stand and to walk on it; then, we will have rest for our souls. (See End Notes for resources to help you keep this balance.) Don't rob your children of these benefits by skipping its teaching because of the difficulty of dealing with death and accountability.

> *Teach your children that God is a loving and merciful Father, but there will be a Judgment Day with everlasting life and everlasting torment.*

Chapter 10

Teach the Children that God is Their Creator

I love Florida! When my children were pre-schoolers, we lived a mile from a wooded park with sandy paths, two slides, and "monkey" bars—all to enjoy in year-round sunshine. We went almost every day with at least one collie in tow. As much fun as all this was, the most lasting effect of those days in the park was this simple little song:

>God made everything.
>God made everything.
>God made everything.

God made the_____(trees, birds, flowers, sky, sun, me…).
>God made_____
>God made everything

Anyone could fill in the blanks so the chorus could go on and on and on. But, the concept of a big God who created all these wonderful delights was ingrained through repetition and rote. These lessons in the park didn't cut the children down or ruin their self-esteem, but they did learn:

- They were created by a person—God.
- The Creator is more magnificent than what He created, the creature. This even included them; they were wonderfully made, but lower than God.

- They had not made themselves or evolved. (Only God is self-existent, the great "I Am.") They glimpsed something of the power, love, and creativity of God and were able, over the years, to see the contrast between themselves and their Creator.
- All things were made to put the focus on God's attributes—for His glory.
- God was to be reverenced.
- A foundation was laid for their seeing themselves as sinners in need of a Savior.

Of course more than trips to the park were needed to teach these concepts. I wish we had done much more repetition and rote learning. But, our "Creation Song" was supplemented by:

> "Who made you?
> God made me.
> What else did God make?
> God made all things.
> Why did God make you and all things?
> For His own glory.
> How can you glorify God?
> By loving Him and doing what He commands."[1]

God as our Creator was a major theme of those pre-school days no matter what we were doing. It is one of those old paths we were trying to dig up and walk upon. Think about some of the ladies from previous chapters. Picture Mary Lee and her daughter, Agnes, looking at a Virginia cotton field or Monica and Augustine enjoying a desert sunset in North Africa or Susie Spurgeon telling her twin boys about the roses in their English garden. Or listen to Fanny Crosby's response to how God had created her:

> O what a happy soul am I
> Although I cannot see,
> I am resolved that in this world

Contented I will be;
How many blessings I enjoy
That other people don't
To weep and sigh because I'm blind,
I cannot, and I won't.²

She wrote these lines when only eight years old in the 1820's in New York long before her first hymns were scrolled. Can't you picture Fanny being kindly instructed in the goodness and creativity of God?

Remind your preschool children and grandchildren of God's attributes revealed in the world all around them—His immense power, His creativity, His love, vastness, and eternal existence. Train them to see God in the flower's detail, the sunrise, the colors of a sunset. You are giving them a life-long reminder of God's presence and involvement in their life. Keep going back to Genesis as they grow older until the concept of Creator contrasted with the created is ingrained in them.

> *"I don't understand why everyone doesn't believe in God when they could just look at these flowers and know He exists."*
>
> Maude Dickinson,
> (Carol's Grandmother)

This takes longer than you think and you will need to remember to delight in childish stages along the way. One time a pastor's three kids were visiting me, their Sunday school teacher. We were looking at each flower in the garden so I started my usual question of "Who made this flower?" Instead of the rote answer back, one creative mind responded, "You did." After a short lesson on seeds and watering, I returned to the question at hand. "Who made the seed?" "The flower did" was the preschool response.

Sometimes it is better to laugh, enjoy the moment, and seek the old paths another day! "How about some lemonade?"

Dr. Martyn Lloyd-Jones, a Welsh medical doctor who preached in London 1938-1968, taught the importance of reverencing God as our Creator:

Let me put it like this to you: if we start with man instead of with God, we are guilty of reversing the biblical order, in our preaching, in our evangelism, in everything else. And I solemnly suggest to you that we are in danger of forgetting God....So you see, it follows that because there is such an inadequate conception of God's love and of the grace of God, and of the holy character and being of God, that is why there is so little true heartfelt praise and joy and thanksgiving....To withhold from the God who has made us anything of ourselves is to sin against Him grievously, and is to merit the punishment and the condemnation of hell![3]

> *"For I say...to everyone who is among you, not to think of himself more highly than he ought to think, but to think soberly..."*
>
> Paul in Romans 12:3

Show them that not to please their Creator offends Him; they are formed by another; they did not make themselves.

Seeing God as his Creator teaches a child humility and awe toward an omnipotent, yet loving God.

Chapter 11

There are Three Aspects to Sin

The study of doctrine by itself is very much like a skeleton drying up in the dust: the bones get brittle, can't move or feel, and finally disintegrate. There is no heart. We don't want that to happen with our devotional lives. So let's make sure we add some devotion and heart to these doctrines.

Pray through Psalm 139. It is full of creation, your uniqueness, and your sin tendency. Don't forget to put on your gospel spectacles; those glasses help you interpret and apply the Old Testament correctly!

Children are so adorable that we all enjoy watching them, especially our own or grandchildren. And each fleeting stage is precious: muscles strengthened enough to flip over; little fingers learning to grasp at the spoon as we feed them; great explorers on the move; four-year-olds singing. It goes on and on! And God created each one for His own glory. *But,*

"There is none righteous, no, not one;
There is none who understands;
There is none who seeks after God.
They have all turned aside;
They have together become unprofitable;
There is none who does good, no, not one.
Their throat is an open tomb;
With their tongues they have practiced deceit;
The poison of asps is under their lips;

Whose mouth is full of cursing and bitterness.
Their feet are swift to shed blood;
Destruction and misery are in their ways;
And the way of peace they have not known.
There is no fear of God before their eyes
(Romans 3:10-18).

For all have sinned and fall short of the glory of God, (Romans 3:23).

The heart is deceitful above all things, And desperately wicked; Who can know it (Jeremiah 17:9)?

Because the carnal mind is enmity against God; for it is not subject to the law of God, nor indeed can be (Romans 8:7).

Even the righteousness of God, through faith in Jesus Christ, to all and on all who believe. For there is no difference; for all have sinned and fall short of the glory of God, being justified freely by His grace through the redemption that is in Christ Jesus (Romans 3:22-24).

There is one body and one Spirit, just as you were called in one hope of your calling; (Ephesians 4:4).

For by grace you have been saved through faith, and that not of yourselves; it is the gift of God, (Ephesians 2: 8).

Do you think children are included? Are they sinners? Do they ever fall short of glorifying God? Can a child experience grace, the unmerited favor of God? Would God give the gift of faith to a young child?

David answered "yes" to these questions in his devotional song in Psalm 51:5-6:

> Behold, I was brought forth in *iniquity*,
> And *in sin* my mother conceived me.
> Behold, You desire truth in the inward parts,

And in the hidden part *You will make me*
to know wisdom.

In *The Geneva Bible* notes, edited by Ludder Whitlock and R.C. Sproul, "yes" is the answer to the above questions:

> The Bible clearly teaches that children are sinners. They are not born innocent and only later become sinners. Children, too, need God's salvation.[1]

Our children should come to the realization that they need a Savior. What we teach them about sin clarifies that need.

> *"Original sin means that sinfulness marks everyone from birth, in the form of a heart inclined toward sin, prior to any actual sins; it is transmitted to us from Adam..."*[2]

Three Aspects of Sin

In Psalm 51:5-6, David was not saying that his mother had sinned sexually or that when she gave birth to him the process was sinful. But, rather, he was referring to the sinfulness that marked his own heart from birth—an inclination he knew well and had specific occasion to lament. As we have seen, Paul taught that "all have sinned and fall short of the glory of God" (Romans 3:23). Paul also believed that this was a mark from birth, (Romans 5:12).

So even our cuddly babies and sweet pre-schoolers playing at the park with joyful abandon have a sin problem that has spoiled their relationship with their Creator.

There is a second aspect of sin that, if you accept it as true will radically affect how you point your child to Jesus. This tendency toward sin, observable in him even now, taints *all* of his person: mind, will, emotions, body. The biblical teaching is that I may not be as bad as I could be, but whatever it is that constitutes "me" is corrupted because of my tendency not to glorify God.

This total sinfulness seeps out through our desires, our mind, conscience, tongue, thoughts, and our actions. See Romans 3:13-15 as well as the following:

> Each one is tempted when he is drawn away by his own *desires* and enticed. Then, when desire has conceived, it gives birth to sin, and sin, when it is full-grown, brings forth death (James 1: 14-15).

> To the pure all things are pure, but to those who are defiled and unbelieving nothing is pure; but even their *mind and conscience* are defiled (Titus1:15).

We need to be reminded, and our children need to be taught, to be wary of our desires, thoughts, even our conscience.

> *"...all becoming dead in sin and wholly defiled in all the faculties and parts of soul and body."3*

Since sin defiles *every* part of our being and is the source of all our actual transgressions, we have *no* ability within ourselves to save ourselves or even to decide to follow God. (This is the third aspect of sin.) That is why even our faith must be a gift from God. There is no spark of good within us that sets us on fire for God or frees our will from this totality of sin. Therefore, salvation must be *all* of grace—God extending mercy to us individually and granting us the means to come to Him.

> *"We...must rely on God...to give them a new inclination that enables them to believe in God, turning from their sins and exercising faith in Christ."*
>
> Carol Brandt

Thus, the third aspect of sin is a logical deduction from total sinfulness. Since our children are marked from birth by sin which impacts them totally, they are without power to believe in God or His word; in a spiritual sense they are dead. They must rely on God, who abounds in mercy and compassion, to give them a new inclination that enables them to believe God, turning from their sin and exercising faith in Christ. They need a new "heart" and a gift of faith. They are unable to repent, believe, or come to Christ by themselves. (See Job 14:4, Jer. 13:23, John 6:33.)

Our culture has rejected all three aspects of sin. Many in conservative Christian circles have rejected or neglected the last two. That has changed their focus away from a gift-bearing, but just God, to a less corrupted child who is able to lift himself out of his "need" by deciding to follow Jesus. But, on the other hand, be careful that you do not become paranoid about this doctrine, twisting it to see the children as evil or childishness as sin. This doctrine is describing their need of a Savior and a work of grace and mercy.

A voice from the past gives us a good example of how to deal with a child regarding his sin. Listen as Frances Havergal, England's consecration poet, writes to children in the 1870's:

> If you had been disobedient and naughty to your dear mother, you would feel that there was something between you and her, like a little wall built up between you. Even though she loved you and went on doing kind things for you as usual, you would not be happy with her; you would keep away from her, and it would be a sorrowful day both for her and for you…
>
> The Lord Jesus knew that it was just like this with us, that there was something between us and God instead of peace, and this something was sin, so of course there never could be any real peace in our hearts. We could never take away this wall of sin; on the contrary, left to ourselves, we only keep building it higher and higher by fresh sins every day. [4]

She uses an everyday experience known to the child to explain how his sins separate him from God. She goes on to explain that only Jesus can cleanse us of our sin by his blood. She even has the child picture the blood of Christ being shed for him.

In today's graphic world, we shudder to mention Jesus's blood to our children. Yet, violence is in all the media. In Vacation Bible School 2000, we taught the "ABC Song" where *admit you're a sinner* wasn't applied personally at all. Instead of being an affront to a loving God deserving of severe punishment, sin was undefined and its remedy was an intellectual agreement that everyone had done "something." And instead of teaching the child that his sinfulness permeates even his will, we sang that salvation was his if he would only *believe and choose*. Confession of sin was omitted. By implication, sin was no longer a barrier since "nothing can separate us from God." The child's inability to save himself wasn't mentioned nor was the need for a work of God's Spirit in his heart. Salvation was as easy as the ABC's. The three aspects of sin, for all practical purposes, had been rejected by a group who proclaimed the inerrancy of Scripture.

There will be plenty of opportunities to teach children their sin, its extent, and their inability to save themselves. Always give the hope of the gospel at the same time you're dealing with sin. The gospel is the power of God to salvation (Romans 1:16). There is hope for us all in Christ Jesus. Teach the children to ask for God's grace to believe and to seek to believe. They need a new heart *and* their duty is to seek God and salvation. One of those mysteries again! It seems contradictory but both are biblical truth. It is another unclear truth. Children need the Savior.

A child taught all three aspects of sin is more likely to grasp his need of a Savior and a work of God's Spirit in his heart.

CHAPTER 12

Keep Your Balance

You're running a marathon. You are used to meeting pressing demands: the baby is wet and hungry; the toddler is getting into the cabinets; the five-year-old wants to have a friend over; then the games begin—soccer, baseball, tennis, etc. etc.!!! A mother's pressures today are quite different from those described by Elizabeth Prentiss in *Stepping Heavenward*. You need muscles and strong bones. Think of doctrine as your bones. Picture your love for God as your muscles. Doctrine, such as the three aspects of sin, gives a framework for your feelings about God—something bones do for the body's flesh. Dry bones are useless but a frame is necessary for strong, muscular action. You need strength in this marathon. That is why doctrine is important.

You may also worry that teaching about sin will cause your child to have such low self-esteem he'll be unable to function in a competitive world. To some it seems when we talk about the child's sin and God's sovereignty in salvation that we're putting the child in a box floating toward destruction, while an unkind God (not to mention unjust), is just letting it happen. We want to give our child a warm hug, reminding him how wonderfully talented he really is, and, "of course, he's made a few mistakes, but he can decide to follow Jesus" and all will be fine. But, to do that, you must reject at least two of those three aspects of sin, and drift away from the teachings of Jesus, Paul and Peter.

So we must find a way to hold fast to Christian teachings without raising beat-down kids. The key is we need to maintain a balance between God's sovereignty in salvation and man's responsibility. The Bible teaches that even though the child is boxed in by sin, he is *free to function according to his tainted nature*. He is not a robot. For example, My cat, Mango, is free to be a a cat. He hunts, crouches, teases my dog. But, he can't be a dog no matter how hard he tries. Mango is free. He is free to act according to his nature. Your child is free to be the sinful little person he is! Yet, he is accountable. Peter uses this same comparison when describing false teachers. They were freely and willfully acting in accordance with their sinful nature, just like a cat or a dog responds according to their natures (See 2 Peter 2:22). And, in a sense, their freedom is limited by that very nature and they become slaves to it unable to act any other way unless God intervenes with grace for them. Therefore, we can look with mercy on these kids yet hold them accountable just as the Bible does.

> *"...we need to teach our children that their freedom is limited by the sin that drags them down, and their only hope is in a compassionate God who delights in giving wonderful gifts..."*
>
> Carol Brandt

That accountablity even affects his self-worth! True self-esteem comes from his learning that God sees him as a free, responsible, gifted child who is dependent on his Creator to overcome the corruption that has become his nature.

In Acts 2:22-23, Peter strengthens our grip on this teaching by blending God's sovereignty and man's responsibility:

> Men of Israel, hear these words: Jesus of Nazareth, a Man attested by God to you by miracles, wonders, and signs which God did through Him in your midst, as you yourselves also know—Him, being delivered by the determined purpose and foreknowledge of God,

> you have taken by lawless hands, have crucified,
> and put to death; (Acts 2:22-23).

Jesus' death was part of the purpose of God but the Jews and Romans were held accountable for their sins of deceit, lying and murder.

My former pastor, Ernest Reisinger, puts it like this:
> If we examine these two truths separately, we will conclude that from Genesis to Revelation the Bible teaches that the God of the Bible is one hundred percent sovereign—sovereign in creation, sovereign in redemption, and sovereign in providence—and that from Genesis to Revelation the Bible teaches that man is one hundred percent responsible for his sin. Therefore, we have no alternative but to believe both are true, even though with our finite minds we cannot reconcile them or harmonize them.[1]

Accountability along with abundant praise result in feelings of self-worth and competency. Seeing your job accomplished well, and rewarded, makes even a child feel good. So teaching your child to recognize his own sins, then praising him when he turns from them and progress is made, leads to increased self-worth but with humility—a child who sees his need of a Savior and His grace.

Another technique to help you run this marathon is prayer. No one is too far gone or too young for the Spirit's work. Encourage your children to pray for a new heart. That prayer is a simple way of asking God to:

1. Convince the child of his/her lost, helpless state.
2. Convict him of his/her sin.
3. Enlighten his/her mind.
4. Renew his/her will.

These are all works of the Holy Spirit.

We have a detailed account, a voice from the past, giving us a glimpse into a child's mind who, apparently, had been taught to pray like this. Agnes Lee was fifteen when she wrote in her journal:

> I know I break God's commandments every minute, all my thoughts are wicked & vain, but this knowledge leaves me there. Time rolls into eternity, & here I stand without being saved, without asking aid.[2]

A year later, in August, 1857, Agnes was assured of her salvation.

> One Sunday evening, I remember it well, for some forgotten cause I did not go to church...I felt so restless, so dissatisfied with myself I could not help being contradictory & disagreeable. I jumped up, went to my own room...God seemed only just and terrible. His glorious presence was always there, but always hidden behind an angry black cloud that ever hung over me...My sins seemed arrayed before me in all their hideousness, I was so low, so insignificant could I dare to imagine God would interest Himself in me....At last the Saviour's, *my* Saviour's words seemed to suit my feelings, 'He that cometh to me I will in no wise cast out.' I clung to that. Gradually hope did come.[3]

This young Virginia girl, daughter of Mary C. and Robert E. Lee, a United States Army officer who later became the hero of the Confederacy, had a sense of her sin and the wall that separated her from God. She knew she needed a Savior and that God's character of love and faithfulness required Him to keep His promises. Her balance came by seeing her responsibility to come to Christ knowing He would keep His promise to save her. Agnes' parents must have maintained this balance between God's work in salvation and their child's responsibility to flee to Christ.

I recently visited the Lee home at Arlington on the Potomac River just across from Washington, D.C.. The National Park Service allows visitors on the grounds and in the house where the Lee family lived. You can stand at Agnes' bedroom door remembering this night in 1857. (A good lesson in the wrongs of revenge is there as well. Walk through the flower garden where you will see the Union soldiers buried on the garden's perimeter after the plantation was confiscated by the United States government. When the Supreme Court righted that wrong and restored the plantation to Mary Lee in the 1870's, no wonder the family decided to sell.) But, Agnes learned of the mercies of God there.

Balance also comes by remembering that these four works of the Holy Spirit greatly differ as to:
1. *Extent* of conviction and enlightening—some may know very little, yet be truly converted and often greater conviction comes after conversion.
2. *Duration*—there is not a given length of time as to conviction, or a given number of days or weeks for enlightening of the mind.
3. *Results*—all true conversions do not produce the same fruit as to usefulness or the amount of zeal. [4]

Remembering this will keep you from suspicion of childhood faith or falling into the pit of granting false assurance.

Another practical technique to hang on this sovereign/responsibility frame is to build habits into the family life-style that utilize the vehicles through which God extends His grace. These include corporate and personal worship, prayer, Bible study, Bible reading, sound preaching, and baptism and the Lord's Supper. Organize your family activities to include all of these regularly.

Biography and history are both tools for teaching that God is in control but man is accountable. Tell, read, or assign "reports" of Bible biographies, family life stories, life of Presidents, or Christian leaders. Discuss how God used Winston Churchill in

World War II, how Rome suffered the consequences of its own moral ineptitude, how Israel ended up as a dispersed people, how God provided for Ruth and Naomi, etc. etc. Point out character traits that led to success or failure. *Do what you can! Stay balanced!*

Think about your appointed task to teach your children or grandchildren about God, your accountability, your own sin and weakness. Then contemplate the majesty, holiness, power, and love of God. Aren't you thankful for His help and for the voices from the past encouraging you to keep on "keeping on."

> ***Keep your balance by gripping these "conflicting" truths together.***

Chapter 13

Teach the Children the Ten Commandments

In Chapter 2, sin was described as all encompassing. Every part of the child's body, mind, and will is directed by the sinfulness that he carries with him from conception. He needs to be recreated and renewed. He is separated from God. He is unable to save himself. Even his ability to make decisions is marred by iniquity within. Without a work of God's Spirit in his heart, he remains unresponsive to the things of God, and in fact, he is hostile toward God, not looking at God as an authority over him; unable to please God. These attitudes show themselves early and unfortunately, increase.

> As the consequence of his fall into a state of sin, man has lost all ability to will the performance of any of those works, spiritually good, that accompany salvation. As a natural (unspiritual) man, he is dead in sin and altogether opposed to that which is good. Hence, he is not able, by any strength of his own, to turn himself to God, or even to prepare himself to turn to God.[1]

That is why your child or grandchild needs a new heart—to be recreated and renewed by God's Spirit; to incline him toward the things of God.

But how can we show him his need of a Savior? And how can we teach children their duties? What exactly is sin anyway? The *Shorter Catechism* defines sin as:

> any want of conformity unto, or transgression of, the law of God. [2]

A Catechism for Boys and Girls puts it even more simply:

> Sin is any transgression of the law of God. What is meant by transgression? Doing what God forbids. [3]

Sinclair Ferguson also simplifies it in *The Big Book of Questions and Answers*, "Sin is thinking, wanting, or doing what displeases God." [4]

Later, he asks the question,

> Where does God teach us what pleases Him? God teaches us what pleases Him in the Ten Commandments. Why does the Ten Commandments tell us what we are not to do? The Ten Commandments tell us what we are not to do because God wants us to avoid spoiling our lives. [5]

So while we're praying for a new heart for our child, we can help him learn how to please God and avoid spoiling his life. He will also see his need of a Savior as he experiences his failure to live up to the demands of the commandments.

Jesus' teachings make it clear that the Ten Commandments apply to all people in all cultures at all times. In Luke 16:14-18, He asserts the stability of the law and explains adultery as including a

> *"The commandments can be regarded as ten protecting friends. What an asset! Ten friends to guard our ways. They go with us into every activity and follow us into every interest. Ten watchmen of our path—these are the Ten Commandments of God. He has set them around us for our sakes because He loves us."*
>
> Ernest Reisinger

casual attitude toward divorce. In Luke 18: 18-29, John 4:7-26, Luke 12 and 14, Jesus uses the Ten Commandments as a moral standard. He does not relegate them to a time and people gone by. Instead, He uses them to expose sin and to reveal the need of His saving mercies.

My daughter, Cari, gives an example of the impact teaching the moral law has on a kindergarten student:

'Thou shalt not lie…thou shalt not lie…thou shalt not lie.' Those powerful words written by Moses in the 20th chapter of Exodus pounded in my mind as I fought the urge to deceive Mrs. Martin. I felt as though I was trapped in the one dimension world of Charlie Brown, and the teacher was blaring her question through the slow harmony of a trombone. 'Cari,' the tortuous tone dragged on, 'where are your glasses? Don't you have to wear them anymore?'

I knew precisely my dilemma, even at the young age of six. I could tell the truth, with the possible risk of being automatically labeled the "four-eyed blonde" of Mrs. Martin's kindergarten class. I could tell a little white lie and pass this possible embarrassing title onto some other poor child more suitable for the part.

My family's daily Bible studies and catechism questions rolled through my mind, attempting to crush all sinful ideas of telling a falsehood to my first teacher. 'What is the ninth commandment?' I heard a voice echoing in my head. Practically answering out loud I said, 'You shall not bear false witness against your neighbor.'

'Good,' said the booming voice resembling my father in his commanding tone, 'What does the ninth commandment teach us?'

'To tell the truth and not speak evil of others.' I heard my older sister respond.

I awoke from the Bible lesson nightmare with the monotone trombone blaring, and fifty beady eyes tearing into my soul in the midst of immense turmoil. 'Cari,' repeated my slightly impatient teacher, 'Where are your glasses? They look very nice on you.'

They look nice on me! Are you kidding? I could have easily avoided the question by crying or throwing a tantrum, but that simply wasn't my style; and besides kindergartners didn't ever perform such preschool-type actions. I simply had to face the issue and answer the question. Combating my conscience that violently fought the poisonous lie, I violated all moral law introduced to me in my six years of existence: 'No, Mrs. Martin, I don't have to wear them anymore.'

> *"My family instructed us in the moral law, and the fact that the infallible word of God should be read and followed—even if it does mean ridicule and name-calling from your peers."*
>
> Cari Brandt

Finally, I felt liberated from the twenty-five pairs of convicting eyes that had the possibility to become professional name-calling enemies. Now that I knew the 'four-eyed blonde' would never have any kind of attachment to my name, I was free to live the normal life of a six year old—or so I thought. I would have gladly accepted the role of the four-eyed weirdo if I had known the punishment awaiting me when my father heard the news of his little girl's deceiving character! [6]

Katharine Willoughby also taught her own children the Ten Commandments and a brief catechism. Because she was a duchess, she was able to require the churches to teach them to the children in her district, Lincolnshire, England. The details of her life grip us as she was caught up in the religious upheavals of England in the 1550's-60's. (Remember Henry VIII, all his wives, and Queen Mary, and Elizabeth? Katharine lived at the same time.) Katharine used her wealth to support the leaders of the reformation and to aid European refugees who fled to England for safety from religious persecution. To believe you were saved from your sins through faith in Christ alone was a dangerous thing. She also put a copy of the English Bible in all the churches in her district, requiring preaching from it. [7]

But, tragedy hit out of the blue. Her college age sons both died within five hours of catching the "sweating sickness." Her response sounds much like Ann Judson, Susie Spurgeon, or Sarah Edwards:

> I give God thanks,...for all His benefits which it hath pleased Him to heap upon me, and truly I take this His last (and to the first sight the most sharp and bitter) punishment not for the least of His benefits, inasmuch as I have never been so well taught by any other before to know His power, His love and mercy, and my own wickedness and the wretched estate that without Him I should endure here... [8]

Katharine, a widow, remarried within two years of her sons' deaths in 1551. But, violent persecution of Protestants began in England. She, her new husband, and infant daughter had a wild escape to Poland via the Netherlands and Germany. Her lands were confiscated, they were robbed and beaten en route, endured a hailstorm out in the open, and finally given protection in Poland for two years. [9] She and her husband were finally able to return to her own lands and raise their two young children in peace. I think she probably taught these "new" children how to use the Ten Commandments to reveal their sin and need of a Savior, don't you?

We, like Katharine, need to answer those same old questions about each of the Commandments: What does it say? What does it mean? How do I apply it? There are several sources to help you:

For an in-depth study of the theology issues behind the moral law read *The Law and the Gospel* (P&R Publishing, New Jersey, 1997). Have you wondered at the decline in its teaching and the nebular definitions of sin? It's because of a schism in evangelical Christianity.

Whatever Happened to the Ten Commandments? by Ernest Reisinger (The Banner of Truth Trust, Edinburgh, 1999) gives general principles for their use and then shows the duty and the sins forbidden by each commandment. *A Catechism For Boys and Girls* (Carey Publications, Great Britain, 1989) puts it in simple language easy to memorize. Sinclair Ferguson includes activities for kids and discussion questions with explanation of each commandment (*The Big Book of Questions and Answers*, Christian Focus Publications, Scotland, 1998).[10]

Use the commandments when you discipline. Be sure the child understands the positive side of the commandment. Discuss how he has sinned and how he can avoid doing it again. Start young and keep at it. *Use the commandment as a teaching tool, not a battering ram. Beware of any paranoid twisting of childishness into evil.* The Shorter Catechism of the Westminster Confession of Faith is a good resource for explaining the positive and the negative ways of keeping the Ten Commandments.[11] Whether y ou are Presbyterian or not, you need this book in your home!

Suppose you catch your four-year-old daughter sneaking into your snack cabinet. She has been warned before that she cannot take those sweets and carbohydrates between meals without your permission. You could show her how this deception is stealing and lying and how both are displeasing to God as well as being disobedient to her parents. To just let it slide by with no comment or correction or punishment is to lose an opportunity to lead her to seeing her need of a Savior as well as how her own heart has led her to sin against her parents and God. But locking her in the closet or thinking she'd be better off dead than so evil as to steal is twisting this into paranoia and misusing something that God meant to be for good.

Remember our comments on remaining balanced and entwining truths? You must always keep love before you as you work and live with and lead children to their sin and Savior. Jesus summarizes the moral law as love for God and others in Matthew 22:34-40, Paul teaches the pre-eminence of love in all human relationships (1 Corinthians 13). Love will restrain you from hammering your kids over the head, from talking about duties and sin to the exclusion of gifts and talents. You will be more kind, patient, enduring while bearing all kinds of childish things (and even fleshly things) because you have hope in the faithfulness and goodness of God. Love for God and others works a wonderful balance as we try to live authentic lives focused on knowing God.

> *The Ten Commandments teach all people everywhere, living at any time, how to please God, how much they need a Savior, and how they have sinned against Him.*

CHAPTER 14

Don't Give Your Child False Assurance

Balance in life is so important. Even the philosophies of the world talk about moderation, energy, and balance. Instead of balancing, we see-saw—up and down, side to side, one extreme to another. Wrong!

We've talked about how the Bible appears to include irreconcilable concepts: sovereignty of God and responsibility of man; humans tainted into their very depth by sin and all being urged to turn from sin, trusting in Christ. Balance is represented by "and;" the see-saw would be "versus." Our lives should include *both* sovereignty *and* responsibility. The contradiction is only an illusion.

Let's look at another area where balance is essential. It has to do with assurance of salvation. Ernest Reisinger defines assurance as:

> ...a God-given conviction of our standing in grace stamped on the mind and heart by the Spirit of God; supernatural discernment of a saving relationship with God. [1]

We can know for sure that we have eternal life. Notice that each individual is urged to seek it; it comes to him consciously from the Holy Spirit—not from his parents, Sunday School teachers, or youth leaders! Granting false assurance to ourselves or someone else is like a see-saw hitting the ground, way out of balance. We always want our children to feel good about themselves and we want to "feel good" ourselves, as well. Instead of urging our children to *seek* assurance on biblical grounds, (2 Peter 1:10, Hebrews 6:11), we pat them on the back reassuring them that since they've asked Jesus into their heart, "of course you're saved; you prayed, didn't you?" We take on the tasks that the Bible reserves for the Holy Spirit.

There are three elements to biblical assurance of salvation. We should base assurance on:

1. The promises of God made alive or real to us by the Holy Spirit. [2] You are promised salvation and being God's child if you believe in Christ in John 1:12-13, Acts 16:31 and John 3:16.

Each person eventually asks: How do I know that I have believed? How do I know that my faith is saving faith? Here is where the Holy Spirit must work in the mind and heart to convince you that each promise is yours. You have believed therefore you are saved. To believe in Christ for salvation is to be persuaded that we shall be saved through His grace. It is a looking to Christ alone, It is exercising faith in Him and what He has promised—that you will have eternal life, because He has granted you faith to believe (Ephesians 2:1-10). Therefore, your hope rests entirely upon Christ, not on your believing or "claiming" the promise. The promise becoming real to you is just the evidence that you have trusted in Christ for the salvation of your soul. For instance, take John 3:16, if you see that you have truly believed and that His blood was shed for *you,* eternal life is yours. That is a promise made real.

2. The second aspect of assurance is the internal witness of the Holy Spirit that causes us to behave towards God as to a Father (Romans 8:12-17). We become assured of our adoption as sons. [3] It is not an immediate testimony or special revelation, but rather an opening of the mind to understand scripture; seeing more of the wonder of Christ and loving Him more. It is not an instant event, but what results from the Holy Spirit's

work in us. It is a very individual thing just as our relationship with God is very personal.

> "The infallible assurance of salvation is not an essential part of salvation, for a true believer may wait for a long time, and struggle with many difficulties, before he attains to it."
>
> The 1689 Confession

One day a friend and I were driving home from a Bible study excitedly rehashing the lesson when she commented that she looked at God as a great King sitting on an unapproachable throne. Every time she tried to pray, this image came into her mind. She thought it strange that I looked up at God as a loving Father to whom I could run with delight being confident of His love and acceptance. I didn't know I was just expressing the evidence of the Spirit's quiet work in my soul. I wonder now whether she has obtained assurance of her own salvation.

Sarah Edwards was apparently converted as a child and even at thirteen her pursuit of God was evidenced in her character. But, at the age of 31, she experienced a time when the promise of God in Romans 8:34 was made so real to her that it stayed with her a long time:

> I was entirely swallowed up in God, as my only portion, and his honour and glory was the object of my supreme desire and delight...and I appeared to myself to float or swim in these bright sweet beams of the love of Christ, like the motes swimming in the beams of the love of Christ... [4]

Don't you know her husband, Jonathan, and the seven children and the household slaves, and visiting theological students enjoyed that year of 1742 as this felt assurance of the favor of God affected her home?

3. The last answer to "How do I know I've believed to the saving of my soul?" is what we see in our own Christian character

and conduct. There are evidences that we have been "made alive" (see Ephesians 2) or "born again." We can see *our* love for Jesus (1 John 5:1). We can observe *ourselves* keeping His commandments (1 John 3:14, 4:7). We can know whether *we* practice being right with God by doing, wanting, thinking what pleases Him (1 John 2:29). These evidences are for our own assurance, not a standard by which we judge others.[5]

Children need the Savior and they need assurances that they are saved. But not from us. We need to avoid that hug and pat on the back coupled with a "Well, of course you're saved. You prayed the prayer, didn't you? You walked down front, remember?" Or "You were baptized and confirmed, weren't you?" Or "Stop worrying, you're a child of the covenant."

Instead, we need to direct them to the promises in the scriptures and pray with them that the Holy Spirit will make those promises real to them. You can inquire if they see God as their dear father in the "Abba, Father" sense. It is also appropriate to point out the evidences of saving faith listed in 1 John. But, that is very different from granting them our assurance that they are saved!

> ***The Holy Spirit is the only one who can give our children evidences that they have truly believed.***

Chapter 15

Avoid Suspicion of Children's Faith

Let's get back on our see-saw and try again. Losing our balance will happen, but we should grow stronger, more resilient and enduring each time.

We are not to falsely assure our children that their believing is real, but on the other hand, we are not to be overly suspicious of childhood faith and love for their Savior. I once attended classes led by a dynamic communicator who had much zeal for God and His kingdom. But, she was convinced that children couldn't really become Christians; they could be instructed in the faith, and later as they approached adulthood, they might become "real" Christians. So she and those who studied with her, were suspicious of any childhood conversions. They soon became suspicious of me, even wondering if I was saved at all, since I couldn't, in good conscience, reject my childhood testimony. Family evangelism and community outreach toward children also suffered because of this suspicion.

Charles Spurgeon recognized this same danger in the 1860's:
> ...the conversion of children is not expected in many of our churches and congregations. I mean, that they do not expect the children to be converted as children. The theory is that if we can impress youthful minds with principles which may, in after years, prove useful to them, we have done a great deal; but to convert children

as children, and to regard them as being as much believers as their seniors, is regarded as absurd. To this supposed absurdity I cling with all my heart. I believe that of children is the Kingdom of God, both on earth and in heaven. [1]

In 2 Timothy 3:10-15, Paul reminds Timothy of his instruction in the scriptures as a boy and of his mother and grandmother's characters and lives lived out before him when he was growing up. Timothy had known the Bible from childhood.

Besides Timothy, David comes to mind as an example of childhood faith. His great-great grandmother, Ruth from Moab, probably did not live to teach him but surely the story of how God provided for Naomi and Ruth was retold in family circles in Bethlehem. I wonder if David's mother and grandmothers taught him the truths of God plainly and simply, making him ready for God's sovereign choice to be King (1 Samuel 16:1-13)?

Then there is Samuel. He was raised by Eli, the priest, but don't you imagine Hannah told him of how God answered her prayer, perhaps teaching him praise songs even before she let him live at the temple? He had an early responsiveness to God and a long life of service and obedience. It is possible to conjecture that the mothers led the way for those childhood conversions. But, God is not limited by our responsibility or lack of it.

A fascinating story is found in 1 Kings 11:26-40, 12:20-33. Jeroboam was raised by his mother, Zeruah, a widow in Israel. We are not told whether she raised him to revere God, or whether she gave him false assurance. But, he disregarded God's commandments by reordering worship to fit his desires. He took the lead in taking Israel down the path of apostasy. His whole family suffered the consequences; all his descendents were killed. We can't make our children believe and obey God, but I wonder if Zeruah was faithful to teach and live a godly life before her son? I wonder if she gave him false assurance? If so, she failed to meet her responsibilities and the consequences affected the whole nation.

Our lack of responsibility does not limit God. His mercies are ever around us. An illustration of this is found in 1 Kings 14:12-13 in Jeroboam's son, Abijah. Abijah lived amidst Jeroboam's idolatry yet "in him is found something good toward the Lord God." If he was totally sinful and unable to turn to God, where did this good come from? Charles Spurgeon connected it to God's grace—an unmerited favor toward Abijah:

> How came this child to have this good thing in his heart? So far we know: we are sure that God placed it there but by what means? The child, in all probability, did not hear the teaching of the prophets of God; he was never, like young Samuel, taken up to the house of the Lord. His mother was an idolatrous princess, his father was among the most wicked of men, and yet the grace of God reached their child.
>
> ...Be it ours when we see in children some good thing to rest content with that truth, even if we cannot tell how it came there. God's electing love is never short of means to carry out its purpose: He can send His effectual grace into the heart of Jeroboam's family, and while the father is prostrate before his idols, the Lord can find a true worshipper for Himself in the King's own child.
>
> ...I should have said let Jeroboam die and his wife too, but spare the child. Ay, but the child must go; he is the fittest. His departure was intended to give glory to God's grace in saving such a child, and making him so soon perfect. It was to be the reward of grace, for the child was taken from the evil to come; he was to die in peace and be buried, whereas the rest of

the family would be slain with the sword and given to the jackals and the vultures to tear in pieces. In this child's case his early death was a proof of grace. ²

We aren't told what means God used to convert Abijah. A household servant? An overheard prayer or song? But, most agree that the usual means of converting a child is through the patient teaching and example of the house where false assurance isn't given, but neither is unwarranted suspicion of children's love tolerated.

Jane Reisinger is another lady of faith who has a story to tell us. Her husband, Ernest, and she raised a son, Don, who never gave them any trouble or indication that his faith was not real faith. They were not suspicious about his childhood faith. Don married, took over the family construction business so Ernest could preach full-time, and had six children in Carlisle, Pennsylvania. But, his life wasn't giving evidence of a relationship with God. His marriage broke up; his six children were left without a father in the home; he remarried; he left the church. And this went on for years and years. Yet, Jane never patted him on the back reminding him of his profession of faith or his baptism or how glad she was that he had it right with God. Instead, she just cried out to God not to let her son go and left his assurance up to the Holy Spirit. She remained silent about it with Don. Don remembers feeling as if he was in an iron cage unable to reach out to God (like in *Pilgrim's Progress*), trapped in his own sin. But, Jane's prayer prevailed and God did not let him go! Can't you hear Jane's voice urging us not to reassure our children that they are saved but to leave that up to God? And telling us not to act suspicious of any child's declaration of faith even though some might leave the faith later.

I can still hear and see two ladies who voiced this suspicion of my faith when I was a child. They whispered, "She's too young to know or understand..." They didn't know that the Holy Spirit had used John 3:16-18 to warm my heart in the realization that there was no condemnation of me since I trusted in Christ. And this warming of my heart came while I was standing on my head memorizing those verses for my Girls' Auxiliary badge! I was still childish, yet being drawn to the Savior.

We've talked about the necessity of using the Ten Commandments to teach our children about their sin. We've looked again at the importance of maintaining assurance and avoiding suspicion of children's faith. Now we're going to look at *five practical helps to leading children* to Jesus:

1. Expect, anticipate, and pray that our children will be saved.
2. Teach them the great truths of the Bible plainly and simply.
3. Labor to arouse their conscience to their sins (as defined by the Ten Commandments) and see their need of a Savior.
4. Seek to excite their minds to ask questions (Deut. 6:20-25).
5. Live before them and tell them of the joy and blessedness of being Christians. [3]

> ***We need to labor diligently for the salvation of our children!***

Chapter 16

Teach the Spiritual Disciplines

Some topics in the last few lessons have been badly maligned in our generation. It is a matter of rediscovering historic Christianity. I hope you're still hanging in there and are increasingly able to sort through any twisted versions of the truth about reverence for God, the three aspects of sin, our accountability in spite of God's sovereignty, the value of the Ten Commandments, and avoiding false assurance or harsh suspicion. This chapter is more concrete, but remember theological abstractions are always foundational to practical living. We want to recover those "lost" doctrines and pass them on to our children.

I cringe when I hear "God is not as interested in your happiness as He is in your godliness." Honestly, deep down I've always wanted happiness. I want my children and husband to be happy. And I've never liked being made to feel guilty for that, or to be forced to choose a miserable godliness. Of course, since our culture is so hedonistic and self-centered, we need reminders that God and His ways are higher than ours. But, it still hits me in the stomach to be told that my Father doesn't care if I'm happy.

Wisdom pays off more than gold or silver jewelry. What do you desire? Rubies? Wisdom is far more precious! And wise living results in "general well-being, harmony, wholeness." [1] Happy are all who hold tightly to wisdom.

We all want this well-being and harmonious wholeness for ourselves and our children. The trick is to find wisdom and gain understanding (Proverbs 3:13-18). How do we equip our children to hold tightly to sound wisdom so that *when* trouble comes their confidence will be in God's favor and His grace? How can they find wisdom?

> *"Happy. The word does not mean merely a subjective feeling. It is found almost exclusively in the Psalms and the wisdom literature, describing the life that enjoys God's grace and favor."*
>
> The New Geneva Bible Notes

One way is to strengthen the equipment that God has given each child. Equipment like a good mind, a desire to learn, a natural curiosity, a quick memory. And we need to teach healthy spiritual disciplines just as we do self-discipline, physical exercise, and getting along with others. Spiritual disciplines give them the tools to find wisdom. They are like exercising in the path of God's grace. [2] So our kids will not only be protected from evil through the right use of the Moral Law, but be in the right place and with the best tools to receive wisdom from above. Exercise is the key. *They must use these spiritual tools regularly, over an extended time*, just as they must use their natural equipment. "Use it or lose it" to quote a secular proverb.

There are some underlying principles of learning that are fundamental here. One is self-discipline; children must be taught to refrain and restrain! Give them a little help so that they restrain themselves and refrain from whatever their age group does to resist learning or direction. Even teens need this! I have no tolerance for youth workers who ignore this principle. Many encourage resistance to authority and promote self-indulgence instead of self-discipline. Self-discipline is a perpetual need for us all.

Another principle for learning is the necessity of focus and concentration upon the task, thought, or skill to be learned.

We're all less focused today because we live with cellular phones, pagers, constant news updates, information saturation etc. An editorial recently in the *Palm Beach Post* called it giving "partial attention" since technology has us at its beck and call. What will that do to successful parenting as well as to each kid's own development? And it is harder yet for children. Give them a little help to concentrate.

Self-discipline and concentration lead us to the other learning skills: how to listen; how to read; how to remember; how to get information. Donald Whitney in *Spiritual Disciplines for the Christian Life* says that the first exercise is "Bible Intake" by hearing, reading, studying, memorization, meditation, and application. Children have to be taught to take in the Bible.

> *"Let us never forget that the message of the Bible is addressed primarily to the mind, to the understanding."*
> Martyn Lloyd-Jones

We all know the importance of reading to our children at an early age and continuing into middle school. Include reading Bible passages out-loud. It trains them to listen, and therefore, really hear the scriptures. It shows them that the Bible is important to you. Repetition of key passages breeds familiarity. Read and re-read aloud passages like Genesis 1, Exodus 20, Psalm 1, Proverbs 3, Luke 2, Matthew 5-7. Children need to hear the scriptures read aloud in our homes. Too often this is not done even in the churches and Sunday schools. One tool you want your children to learn to use is that of hearing God's word. It is a channel or path of God's grace to them. [3]

Donald Whitney lists ten spiritual disciplines: Bible Intake, prayer, worship, evangelism, disciplined serving, stewardship, fasting, silence and solitude, journaling, intentional learning (especially through reading). He recommends doing all these things for the purpose of growing more like our Lord Jesus Christ. [4] Think about ways you could foster these in your children or grandchildren. And how you can circumvent their natural resistance to disciplining themselves. For instance, we're all familiar with church nursery introductions to prayer and Bible intake. But, my experience has been that we often drop the ball as the children mature. Gently introduce your preschooler to church worship, giving him a little help to focus and participate. Sit close; share your hymnal with that second grader even if she can't pronounce all the words. I'm a terrible artist but I tried to illustrate the sermon points as we listened together. Foster a sense of reverence for the majesty of God and the blessings of worshiping Him in your preschool or early elementary child.

I've already mentioned my reaction to youth leaders who foster self-indulgence. Many do a wonderful job of introducing service with leaf raking or gutter cleaning for the older members of the congregation. But, we need to nurture the discipline aspect of serving others in our homes. Teens need to learn that serving is a part of loving others even when it isn't fun. Brainstorm with a friend on ways that could be done.

Don Whitney teaches that fasting can be done in a variety of ways but always for the purpose of using hunger as a call to prayer. Use common sense here. For teens, a juice fast for a

> *"Moreover, when you fast, do not be like the hypocrites, with a sad countenance. For they disfigure their faces that they may appear to men to be fasting. Assuredly, I say to you, they have their reward. But you, when you fast, anoint your head and wash your face, so that you do not appear to men to be fasting, but to our Father who is in the secret place, and your Father who sees in secret will reward you openly."* —Matthew 6:16-18

morning or other limited hours might be appropriate with the objective of praying for a special need or guidance.

I was introduced to the value of silence and solitude at a youth weekend retreat. We were instructed to find a pastoral setting to pray, read scripture, and think about God *alone*. It reinforced my mother's modeling of personal prayer and Bible reading. And at a youth conference that I attended with *my* children, everyone had to get alone to read a designated portion of scripture each day. But, this can be incorporated into our families as well. Even upper elementary children could do this in short spans. The point is to understand the developmental stage of your child and introduce these tools. Don't be put off by their resistance; it is only natural. They can use these tools for life!

I used a "Drop Everything and Read!" concept several summers with my children. No matter what any of us were doing (including me!), at a special signal everyone had to stop what he was doing and start reading. Even young teens could continue this. And the reading could include wonderful biographies of Christians read aloud or silently. But the discipline of intentional learning would be introduced.

Now for a sad story. Zeruiah was King David's sister, reared in Jesse's household of eight sons and two daughters. She had three sons: Joab, Abishai, and Asahel. They fought for their Uncle David. Joab even became the commander of the King's army.

While rearing her children, Zeruiah must have made some effort to strengthen their natural "equipment" by emphasizing a healthy lifestyle of exercise, good eating habits, keeping fit. After all, they became leaders of David's mighty men. But, did Zeruiah teach the spiritual disciplines so they could acquire wisdom, applying truths to life and thus becoming men of moral excellence as well? We aren't told, but we are given glimpses into their character—or lack of it (see 2 Samuel 18-19). Joab showed no moral courage when he went along with David's plot against Uriah. He put Uriah in the place of certain death. He killed the leader of Saul's army, Abner, and his own cousin, Amasa. Joab was shrewd and worldly. He manipulated David into allowing the murderer, Absalom, to return to Jerusalem from which he organized his rebellion against his father (2 Samuel 14-15). Later, Joab thrust three spears right through Absalom's heart in disregard to David's order to let him live. That death penalty could have been out of revenge and jealousy rather than a sincere desire to prevent further rebellion (see 2 Samuel 17: 23).

David voices his own frustration with all of Zeruiah's sons, "What have I to do with you, you sons of Zeruiah, that you should be adversaries to me today?" (2 Samuel 19:22). Even though fewer details are given about Asahel and Abishai, David links the three together as his enemies. Were they his enemies when he sought to do right? From his deathbed, David orders Solomon to execute Joab, knowing that Solomon's reign would not be secure as long as this crafty, self-seeking nephew lived! Do you think these brothers had peace, joy, a sense of well-being, happiness and wisdom?

Guess who gets the credit for raising these men? Zeruiah. Their father is never mentioned! Perhaps I'm overreacting; the writer of this history may have just wanted to show their kinship with David. We don't know any details of their family life, but I wonder if Zeruiah emphasized the spiritual disciplines when her boys were young. What do you think her voice from the past would tell us?

The purpose of this chapter is to focus us on the need for equipping ourselves and our children with the skills to reap spiritual blessings and rediscover historic Christianity. Notice that this process is not "Let go and let God," but "Get up and get going!" It's that balance thing again—balancing God's sovereignty and our responsibility/duty. It takes effort, planning, and commitment on our part.

> *Train children to use and value the spiritual disciplines*

CHAPTER 17

Teach the Great Truths Plainly and Simply

In the last chapter, we talked about teaching our children to practice the spiritual disciplines so they will walk in wisdom. We want them to have a life of harmonious wholeness just as in the Jewish blessing of "shalom." Of course, spiritual disciplines are nothing more than a means or path through which God's grace can be experienced, His wisdom obtained, and therefore, this harmony and wholeness enjoyed. They are the old paths on which historic Christianity will be rediscovered.

I hope you have already started your own exercise program, and one for your children, that will put you in Jesus' path strengthened to receive His mercy and unmerited favor. Remember, these disciplines don't make you or your child better than others or more right with God. Only faith in Christ alone makes you right with God. While you are "working out," remember that the great truths of the *Bible* can be taught simply and plainly.

> *"I do hold that there is no doctrine of the Word of God which a child, if he be capable of salvation, is not capable of receiving."*
>
> Charles Spurgeon

The summary truths of the Christian faith such as creation, sin, atonement, judgment, providence, and sovereignty can be taught without complexity by using some easy techniques and tools.

In 1884, Dr. John Milton Gregory published *The Seven Laws of Teaching*. He was the founding president of the University of Illinois, a Baptist minister and educator. His little book was "especially successful as a handbook for Sunday school teachers."[1] The following list is my application of Dr. Gregory's "laws" to teaching Bible truths.

1. **A teacher must be one who knows the lesson or truth or art to be taught.** [2] You must understand the biblical truth you're teaching.

    You need to know what you believe. You need to bone up on the basics. You do not need a theology degree, but you should sit under sound preaching and teaching. You should have a grasp of those summary truths of Christianity as revealed in all of scripture.

2. **Use their language as they use it.** Keep it simple. We are not talking about crudeness; learn how they use words. This requires you to do some listening (especially grandmothers) so you know how children and teens are talking. A mouse clicks today! Communicate eternal truths through a changing language. Teach the concept first before getting into new terminology. For instance, don't worry whether they can spell "providence" until they grasp the concept of a powerful God who controls the universe out of His love and wisdom. A child can learn wise, good, and powerful but may miss the whole idea if you concentrate on providence and sovereignty.

3. **"A learner is one who attends with interest to the lesson."** [3]

    To attend to the lesson is an old fashioned way of saying to pay attention. And Mr. Gregory added "with interest." It was (and still is) the child's responsibility to pay attention and be interested. Our society has let that responsibility slip away from the child to the teacher who must entertain. We should hold them accountable, but it is wise to give them a little help.

I recently attended a Child Evangelism Fellowship harvest party where a gifted teacher tried unsuccessfully to convey some wonderful truths using visual aids and personal attractiveness, while some of the kids wandered around, talked to each other, or watched the cat. Remember it is harder for children to focus today. Give them a little help. When I'm not in Florida, I'm in a small town in western Kentucky where they know how to give a child a little help. Children are treasured there; the adults show it by the way they relate to the kids, with afffection, warmth, and a hands on involvement; they're not in the way or a burden. So when discipline or structure is needed, that help is more readily accepted.

4. **Use the known to teach the unknown.** One of the best examples of this is the song "God is so big, so strong and so mighty, there's nothing my God cannot do." Children usually know by age two what big and strong mean. This song uses the known to teach about God's sovereignty (no need to get into the term!) and expand the child's vocabulary to include mighty. So ask yourself: "What do they already know that I could use to teach this truth?" it doesn't have to be "religious" to be a springboard for truth. For example, do the children see chipmunks scampering under a boulder? You could teach that God is our refuge—a safe hiding place for us like under the rock is for the chipmunks.

5. **Stimulate their mind's characteristics to grasp the desired truth.** Those characteristics are: the love of mimicry, curiosity, doubt, organization, critical selection and rejection, memory, imagination, and application. This is part of the equipment God gives each of us. You want their mind to work. Begin with mimicry and memory.

This is where catechism questions and memory verses come in. Rote is a mental process. But don't stop there. Curiosity and imagination—even doubt—can be useful for understanding truths too. Dr. Gregory tells us, "Do not rest until each child shows his mental activity by asking questions." [4]

Remember the three questions to ask while studying (or teaching) the Bible?

What does the passage say?
What does it mean?
How do I apply it?

Notice how these questions engage the mind and lead to the heart. Use them to stimulate thinking that leads to knowledge, understanding, and wisdom which results in true happiness.

6. **"Learning is thinking into one's own understanding a new idea or truth, or working into habit a new art or skill."** [5] The teacher is to stimulate the mental processes; the learner is to exercise those processes. (Humans are always responsible and accountable!) When you've given your all, the child must increasingly do his part. You can't make his brain work nor are you accountable if he refuses. But, you can ask some questions at his level that will require or prod him to think. Don't tolerate laziness or stupor.

7. **Review, rethink, reproduce, apply.** Application makes the truth personal and useful. For example, since you are created by a loving and strong God, should you look at yourself as ugly or with nothing to offer? Application reaches the whole person, engaging the emotions, the will, as well as the mind. Knowing God and increasing in holiness should be our ultimate desires for ourselves and our children.

Review and repetition are crucial for retention. Simple questions and answers work! Rethinking a concept opens up new elements we never noticed before. That's why we can come back again and again to the Bible truths. And they can be taught simply and plainly. Even the great mysteries.

A voice from the past speaks to us on this point. Frances Ridley Havergal wrote *Little Pillows* because:

> ...even little hearts are sometimes very weary, and want something to rest upon; and a happy little heart, happy in the love of Jesus, will always be glad to have one of His own sweet words to go to sleep upon. [6]

Frances also wrote *Morning Bells* as "little chimes of Bible music to wake you up!" [7] She could take a doctrinal truth and put it into the child's own words making it plain and simple. To teach Ephesians 1:6 that believers are "accepted in the Beloved," she tells a story of a king who invited a poor child to live in his palace:

> Suppose you heard this, and wished the king would take you. Then the king beckons you, and you venture near; and then the prince royal himself comes and leads you up to his father, and tells you to say what you want, and you say, 'I do want to go, please take me!' Will the king break his word and not take you?...So every one who has come to Jesus, even if only a little girl or boy, is "accepted in the Beloved." Accepted, because God has said, 'I will receive you.' Accepted, because He Himself has called you and drawn you, or you never would have wanted to come.[8]

Frances lived in England 1836-1879, was educated in Hebrew and Greek and other modern languages and trained as a concert soloist and pianist. Instead, she taught Sunday School, wrote hymns like "I Gave My Life For Thee" and "Who Is On the Lord's Side" and leaflets and little books for children. Hear her voice telling us to teach the truths plainly and simply; don't avoid the great truths as too difficult for children. If you do, you might raise children who aren't connected to historical Christianity at all.

I can't get Zeruiah and her three sons off my mind. Why is she mentioned so many times in 2 Samuel and 1 Chronicles? Perhaps her relation to David was important to tell, but I keep wondering about her parenting skills. Did she teach the truths about sin, the need for moral courage, the Ten Commandments, the hope of the Messiah as an atonement for sin? Or was she rushing around organizing practices and lessons in handling a sword, muscle development, and showing courage in battle? Did she teach the great biblical mysteries plainly and simply to her sons? I doubt it. She probably didn't have time.

And don't forget to keep checking your own attitudes as you go in and out through your day with the hope of leading your children or grandchildren to God: "…we dealt with each of you *as a father deals with his own children, encouraging, comforting, and urging* you to live lives worthy of God." 1 Thessalonians 2:11. "We were gentle among you, *like a mother caring for her little children.*" 1 Thessalonians 2:7.

Seven principles of teaching help us to pass God's truths to the next generation—plainly and simply.

CHAPTER 18

Keep Your Tools Handy

Practicing spiritual disciplines puts you in the "place" where you can be blessed. Using instructional techniques around the home helps build a body of Christian knowledge that can be used by God to impact your child's heart. In our attempt to "get up and get going" with this task of evangelizing our children, we need to keep some tools handy. You will need to grab your "tools" at the most inopportune moments while raising a family. The following is my purely subjective "tool list" gained from my experience and library. "Handy" is the operative term!

1. **Prayer.** What will be the results of disciplines, instructional techniques, and tools without God's work in each life? I don't love dusting and vacuuming! But, I found that the quiet times spent cleaning could be redeemed by praying. Cleaning house became a reminder to pray for each of the children and my husband, John. Since we've allowed our collies (four in all but never more than two at a time!) and cats to go freely in and out of the house, I've had plenty of calls to prayer! Wash your efforts in prayer.

2. **Parent's example.** Your lives are an open book that your children will read even in the age of computers and videos. Practice what you "preach". Repent. Serve. Love God and your neighbors.

3. **Confessions of Faith and catechisms.** In previous chapters, I've already tried to show you the value of grabbing *your*

confession of faith for quick reference or study so you'll know what you're teaching. Catechisms can equip you and your children.

Simple questions with clear and plain answers help in the rote phase of learning, can be easily reviewed, and with the proper questioning can lead to engaging the understanding and critical thinking skills. Dr. Tom J. Nettles, a professor at The Southern Baptist Seminary in Louisville, Kentucky, recommends this tool, "As a hedge against heresy and a wedge to open the mind to truth, the catechism serves as a valuable spiritual tool."[1] And they can be kept handy (on top of the refrigerator?).

> *"Catechizing does to the preaching of the word the same good office that John the Baptist did to our Savior; it prepares the way, and makes its path straight, and yet like him does but say the same things."*
>
> Matthew Henry

Mrs. Mary C. Lee, while with her husband, Robert E., at West Point Military Academy in New York before America's Civil War, requested her mother look around in Washington and Alexandria for catechism books:

> I send you $2 of our Society money with which I want you to get, as far as it will go, some first and second reading books and some of a very small catechism called *Brown's Catechism* commencing with 'Who made you? God. Who redeemed you? Christ. Who sanctifies you? The Holy Ghost.' I believe you know it, we had it at Arlington. [2]

Can't you hear her voice from the past urging us to rediscover those old catechisms, using that old path to instruct our children in the basics of historical Christianity?

Don't fall into the trap of listening to those who malign catechizing. They frequently are from one of three camps. Those who believe that reason is the finale criteria for determining truth reject the rote aspects of catechizing. Those who believe that spiritual experience determines truth fear that rote and repetition will result only in a cold orthodoxy. And post-modernists currently reject catechizing because their focus is on fulfilling individual desires or what Dr. Nettles calls "the absoluteness of me." [3]

> "For my part, I am more and more persuaded that the study of a good Scriptural catechism is of infinite value to children...Even if the youngsters do not understand all the questions and answers... Yet, abiding in their memories, it will be of infinite service when the time of understanding comes to have known these very excellent, wise and judicious definitions of the things of God..."
>
> C. H. Spurgeon

The Confessional Christianity tradition has promoted the use of catechisms for children and new believers since the 1500's. (The Westminster Shorter Catechism was used by the Presbyterians and was almost the same as the Savoy Confessional of the Congregationalists.) There are strong links to this tradition in the Southern Baptist Convention, as well as the Presbyterian Church in America. The Baptist Catechism (also called Keach's Catechism) of about 1693 defined "Baptist" throughout the 1700's and into the 1800's. It was reprinted by Charles Spurgeon in 1855. It had been reprinted in 1813 by the Charleston Association of Baptist churches. The Sunday School Board of the Southern Baptist Convention selected John Broadus, president of Southern Seminary, to write a catechism made up of fifteen lessons with questions for basic and advanced children.[4] Catechisms have a long tradition in American protestant churches and homes.

I used *A Catechism For Boys and Girls* because it was simple. I used the Westminster Shorter Catechism for more depth and for my own reference. We learned along with the kids. After all, this has been a rediscovery process for us. Perhaps it is for you. See the end notes for additional resources.[5]

4. **Visual pictures.** Using words that bring a concrete object or picture to mind and relating this to a spiritual concept is an invaluable tool. Jesus and the prophets did it all the time. It uses the known to teach the unknown. It stimulates the imagination and curiosity. It uses the language of the learner (those teaching techniques again!). The girls and I spent a lot of time at the beach. We would find snails clinging to the cleft of the rock which I said was like holding on to Jesus for protection, salvation, refuge. Jesus was the cleft in the rock, the Rock of Ages. The key is to go from known concrete to spiritual concept—*like* this, *like* that. The only problem was my pre-schoolers had no clue what the word "cleft" was which I used all the time. (I was trying to expand their vocabulary! Not a good idea in this case.) I should have gone from snail to us. "Look how the snail clings to the rock *like* we should cling to Jesus to save us and guard us." The person or child must be familiar enough with the concrete example so an immediate picture comes to mind.

Frances Havergal used this tool all the time. In her book, *Little Pillows,* even the title is a visual picture.

> So here are thirty-one 'little pillows,'...Read the little book before you kneel down to say your evening prayers, because I hope what you read will always remind you of something to pray about. And then, when you lie down and shut your eyes, let your heart rest on the 'little pillow' till 'He giveth His beloved sleep.'[6]

Why not give a copy of *Little Pillows* along with a child's pillow and pillow case to the child in your life?

It would help you to come up with five word *pictures from your child's own experience* that would teach a spiritual truth. You might make a relevant list for each child in the family depending on age and experiences. Keep the list handy. Repeat it. Ask questions that would stimulate his thinking and hopefully he'll ask questions back! As he matures, come up with another list.

A special word to Grandmothers. This is a wonderful way for you to teach and evangelize while building memories at the same time. Keep your list handy and up-to-date with the grandchild's experiences and vocabulary.

5. **Proverbs.** They are plain and simple. They relate the concrete to the spiritual. They motivate. They are quick! They are easy to memorize. They deal with the child's real world. I kept this tool handy by using *Signposts From Proverbs* by Rhiannon Weber (Banner of Truth, Great Britain, 1988). It was on top of the refrig too!

6. **Resources and Methods.** Start your own folder. (See the End Notes at the end of this study for help with resources. I have included phone numbers and e-mail addresses for fast delivery.) There are a lot of helps out there, but don't let the simple basics get swallowed up or pushed aside. You only have so much time, money, and concentration.

> *"Concern for conversion and fervor…should never diminish one's commitment to the individual truths of Christianity nor the necessity of teaching them in a full and coherent manner."*
>
> Tom Nettles

"Train up a child in the way he should go, and when he is old, he will not depart from it." Proverbs 22:6

Tools for teaching and evangelizing a family need to be kept handy.

CONCLUSION

Listen to the voices…
    Rediscover the old paths…
        Walk on the old paths where others have walked…
            Remember God's promises…
                Redirect those little feet…

End Notes

Many of the following resources could be helpful to you. Therefore, easy ordering information is included where known.

Chapter 1 – Love and Enjoy Your Children

1. Faculty Wives Cookbook: A Collection of Recipes from the Southern Baptist Theological Seminary Family, (Morris Press, 1997), p.5.
2. Spurgeon, C.H. *Come Ye Children*, (Christian Focus Publications, Scotland, 1994), p. 85.

Chapter 2 – Providence Dispels Fears

1. James, Sharon. *My Heart In His Hands*, (Evangelical Press, Durham, England, 1998), p. 15.
2. James, Sharon, p. 95.
3. James, Sharon, p. 178-79.
4. Whitlock, Luder and Sproul, R.C., (ed) *New Geneva Study Bible*, (Thomas Nelson Publishers, Nashville, 1995), p. 1934.
5. *The Baptist Confession of Faith of 1689*, (Grace Baptist Church, Carlisle, Pennsylvania), p. 15. (Order your copy from The Christian Gospel Book Service, 1-941-549-3021)
6. *The Baptist Faith and Message*, (Sunday School Board of the Southern Baptist Convention, 1963), p.8.

Chapter 3 – The Providence of God is Sweet

1. Schooland, Marion. Leading Little Ones To God, (W. B. Eerdmans Publishing Co., Grand Rapids, Mi., 1962), p.59.

Chapter 4 – What We Believe Shapes Our Character

1. Ray, Charles. *Mrs. C.H. Spurgeon*, (Pilgrim Publications. Pasadena, Texas 1979), p. 16 (originally published 1903).
2. Spurgeon, C.H. *Autobiography Vol. II*, (Pilgrim Publications, Pasadena, Texas, 1992), p. 291-292. (originally published 1897).
3. Packer, J.I. "The Challenge of the Third Millennium," *Reformed Quarterly*, Summer 1999, p. 10.
4. James, Sharon. *My Heart In His Hands*, p. 203.
5. James, Sharon. p. 203
6. Packer, J.I. "Millennium," p. 11.

Chapter 5 – Grabbing At Straws

1. Nettles, Tom J., "Confession: A Union of Heart Between Sheep and Shepherd." *Founders Journal*, 49/19, Summer, 2002.
2. The Baptist Confession of Faith of 1689, p. 7.
3. Reisinger, Ernest. "Are Creeds and Confessions Divisive?" *Good News*, (North Pompano Baptist Church, February 29, 1984), p. 15. (His writings are available from Christian Gospel Book Service, 1-941-549-3021)

Chapter 6 – Your Commitment Determines Your Reaction to Resistance

1. Weber, Rhiannon. *Signposts From Proverbs*, (Banner of Truth Trust, Carlisle, Pennsylvania, 1988), p. 46. Order from Cumberland Valley Book Service, 1-800-656-0231

2. Brandt, Dr. Henry and Skinner, Kerry. *I Want To Enjoy My Children,* (Life Change, West Palm Beach, Florida), p. 113-114. (Dr. Brandt is no relation to my husband, John. We heard him speak many times in the 1980's. Copies of this are still available from First Baptist Church, West Palm Beach, Fl., www.fbcwpb.org or 1-561-650-7400.)
3. Rose Mortimer E. MacDonald. *Mrs. Robert E. Lee,* (American Foundation Publications, P.O. Box 752, Stuart Drafts, Va., 1998), p. 293
4. Faith Cook. *Singing in the Fire,* (Banner of Truth Trust, Carlisle, Pennsylvania), p. 73

Chapter 7 – Children Need to See Your Fear of God

1. Packer, p. 11
2. Vine, W.E. *An Exposition Dictionary of New Testament Words,* (Fleming Revell Company, New Jersey, 1940), p. 84

Chapter 8 – Practical Hints for Instilling Reverence

1. Whitlock and Sproul, p. 503
2. Spurgeon, C.H. *Come Ye Children,* (Children Focus Publications, Scotland, 1944), p. 123
3. Spurgeon, C.H. *Come Ye Children,* p. 119

Chapter 9 – Check Your Grip

1. Spurgeon, C.H. *Come Ye Children,* p. 100
2. Spurgeon, C.H. *Come Ye Children,* p. 101
3. *Westminster Confession of Faith,* (Bell and Bain, Ltd., Glasgow, 1995), p. 122-125. (Order from The Christian Gospel Book Service, 1-941-549-3021)
4. *The 1689 Confession,* (Carey Publications, Great Britain, 1997), p. 64-65. (Available from Christian Gospel Book Service, 1-941-549-3021)

5. *The 1689 Confession Study Guide* is available from Mt. Zion Bible Institute, www.TheBibleInstitute.org

Chapter 10 – Teach Children that God is Their Creator

1. *A Catechism for Boys and Girls,* (Carey Publications, Great Britain, 1989), p. 5
2. Loveland, John. *Blessed Assurance,* (Broadman Press, Nashville, Tenn., 1978), p. 22-23
3. Martyn Lloyd-Jones. *Romans: The Gospel of God,* (Zondervan, Grand Rapids, Michigan, 1985), p. 362-363. Order from Cumberland Valley Book Service, Carlisle, Pennsylvania (1-800-656-0231)

Chapter 11 – Teach All Three Aspects of Sin

1. Whitlock, Luder and Sproul, R.C., (ed) *New Geneva Study Bible,* (Thomas Nelson Publishers, Nashville, 1995), p. 808
2. *The Baptist Confession of 1689,* (Carey Publications, Great Britain, 1977), p. 64-65. (Available from Christian Gospel Book Service, 1-941-549-3021)
3. *The Baptist Confession of 1689,* p. 16
4. Havergal, Frances, *Little Pillows,* (Reiner Publications, Swengel, Pa. 17880, 1976), p. 25-26. (This volume is now available from Solid Ground Christian Books along with its companion volume, *Morning Bells.* You can order by calling them toll free at 1-877-666-9469 or on-line at http://solid-ground-books.com) She uses wonderful word pictures of spiritual principles to be read by or to children. You could learn how to use familiar images to teach spiritual concepts.

Chapter 12 – Keep Your Balance

1. Reisinger, Ernest C. *God's Will, Man's Will, and Free Will,*

(Mt. Zion Publications, Pensacold, Florida), p. 39. (All Pastor Reisinger's writings may be ordered from The Christian Gospel Book Service, 1-941-549-3021, or ordered directly from Mt. Zion Publications, www.mountzion.org or 2603 W. Wright St., Pensacola, Fl. 32505.)
2. MacDonald, Rose M., Appendix, "Will I Ever be a Christian? A Spiritual Journey to Forgiveness: From the Journal of Agnes Lee, p. 304
3. MacDonald, p. 304
4. Reisinger, Ernest C. *Today's Evangelism*, (Craig Press, Phillipsburg, New Jersey, 1982), p. 42
5. Keeping your balance is such a problem. What you use for your own devotionals is crucial. I have noticed that those who consistently read the following authors tend to stay balanced in their doctrinal application showing less arrogance and more mercy toward others and more love for God: Matthew Henry, especially his *Bible Commentary;* William Jay, *Morning Exercises;* Charles Spurgeon, *Morning and Evening;* sermons by Martyn Lloyd-Jones. It is interesting to note that William Jay read Matthew Henry, Charles Spurgeon read Jay and Henry, and Martyn Lloyd-Jones read them all. Ernest Reisinger read from all these men. Order from Cumberland Valley Book Service, 1-800-656-0231.

Chapter 13 – Teach the Ten Commandments

1. *The Baptist Confession of 1689,* p. 31. (Order from Christian Gospel Book Service, 941-549-3021)
2. *Westminster Confession of Faith,* (Bell and Bain, Ltd., Glasgow, 1995), p. 122-125. (Order from The Christian Gospel Book Service, 1-941-549-3021), p. 290
3. *A Catechism for Boys and Girls,* p. 7
4. Ferguson, Sinclair B. *The Big Book of Questions and*

Answers, (Christian Focus Publications Ltd., Scotland, 1998), p. 18
5. Ferguson, Sinclair B. p. 51-52
6. Brandt, Cari. A class assignment at Palm Beach Atlantic College, West Palm Beach, Fl., 1999.
7. Alexander, J.H. *Ladies of the Reformation,* (Gospel Standard Strict Baptist Trust, 1978), p. 110
8. Alexander, J.H., p. 111
9. Alexander, J.H., p. 113
10. Order these books from the publisher or from Cumberland Valley Bookstore, Carlisle, Ps., 1-800-656-0231.
11. *Westminster Confession of Faith, p.* 180-237

Chapter 14 – Don't Give Your Child False Assurance

1. Reisinger, Ernest C. *Today's Evangelism,* p. 115-116
2. Reisinger, Ernest C. *Today's Evangelism,* p. 122
3. Reisinger, Ernest C. *Lord and Christ* (P&R Publishing, New Jersey, 1994), p. 120-121. (Based on the teaching of Jonathan Edwards. Order from The Christian Gospel Book Service, 1-941-549-3021)
4. Murray, Iain H. *Jonathan Edwards,* (The Banner of Truth Trust, Carlisle, Pennsylvania, 1987), p. 195
5. *Assurance of Salvation* by Ernest C. Reisinger is out of print. Contact The Christian Gospel Book Service (1-941-549-3021) to see if republication is possible. This is a very valuable little book.

Chapter 15 – Avoid Suspicion of Children's Faith

1. Spurgeon, *Come Ye Children,* p. 11-12
2. Spurgeon, *Come Ye Children,* p. 134ff
3. Ernest Reisinger, "The Family and Evangelism," (Banner of Truth Magazine).

Chapter 16 – Train Children to Use the Spiritual Disciplines

1. *New Geneva Bible,* p. 928
2. Whitney, Donald S. *Spiritual Disciplines For the Christian Life,* (Navpress, Colorado Springs, 1977), p. 17. Order from Cumberland Valley Book Service, 1-800-656-0231.
3. Whitney, Donald S. *Spiritual Disciplines for the Christian Life,* p. 89
4. Whitney, Donald S. *Spiritual Disciplines for the Christian Life,* Table of Contents

Chapter 17 – Teach the Great Truths Plainly and Simply

1. Gregory, John Milton. *The Seven Laws of Teaching,* (Baker House, Grand Rapids, 1992), Preface. (This is a reprint from the original 1888 edition including the changes made in 1917.)
2. Gregory, John Milton. *The Seven Laws of Teaching,* p. 18
3. Gregory, John Milton. *The Seven Laws of Teaching,* p. 18
4. Gregory, John Milton. *The Seven Laws of Teaching,* p. 100
5. Gregory, John Milton. *The Seven Laws of Teaching,* p. 19
6. Havergal, Frances. *Little Pillows,* p. 7
7. Havergal, Frances. *Little Pillows,* p. 8
8. Havergal, Frances. *Little Pillows,* p. 12-13

Additional Resources:
- *Truth and Grace Memory Book I* and *Memory Book II* and *The Baptist Catechism Set to Music CD* guide you from age 2–grade 8 on memory verses, catechism questions, and hymns. Order from Solid Ground Christian Books, www.solid-ground-books.com or call toll free 1-877-666-9469.
- Susan Hunt, education coordinator for Presbyterian Church in America, has written a book on teaching the Shorter Catechism to children. Contact Cumberland

Valley Book Service at 1-800-656-0231 or Legacy
Christian Education Publications at 1-800-283-1357.

Chapter 18 – Keeping Your Tools Handy

1. Nettles, Tom J. *Teaching Truth, Training Hearts*, (Calvary Press, Amityville, New York, 1998), p. 53. Order from Christian Gospel Book Service, 1-941-549-3021)
2. MacDonald, Rose. *Mrs. Robert E. Lee*, p. 293.
3. Nettles, Tom J. *Teaching Truth, Training Hearts*, p. 14
4. Nettles, Tom J. *Teaching Truths, Training Hearts*, p. 183-222.
5. *Truth and Grace Memory Book I* and *Memory Book II* guide you from age 2 – grade 8 on memory verses, catechism questions, and hymns. (Order from Founders Press, www.orders@founders.org or P.O. Box 150931, Cape Coral, Fl. 33915
6. Havergal, Frances. *Little Pillows*, p. 7-8. (Order from Solid Ground Christian Books at solid-ground-books.com or call 1-877-666-9469)

Other Related SGCB Titles

Little Pillows and Morning Bells by Frances Ridley Havergal
This is the volume mentioned several times in this book. It is one of the finest books to read with young children at the close and the start of every day. Miss Havergal loved children and wrote in such a way that enabled them to grasp difficult concepts by use of familiar images and examples. A heart-warming little volume.

The Pastor's Daughter: *The Way of Salvation Explained to a Young Inquirer from Reminiscences of the Conversations of her Father, Rev. Edward Payson* by Louisa Payson Hopkins
This volume grants us a rare glimpse into the household of the Payson family of Portland, Maine in the early 1800's, as Edward Payson's oldest daughter recalls the patient and loving way her father led her to true conversion over a period of more than 10 years, from 4-14.

Stepping Heavenward by Elizabeth Payson Prentiss
This volume has touched and changed the lives of hundreds of thousands of women all over the world since the day it was first published in 1869. It is a favorite of such ladies as Martha Peace, Elisabeth Elliot, Susan Hunt, Joni Eareckson Tada, Kay Arthur and many, many more. Both women and men will love it!

The Young Lady's Guide: *to the Harmonious Development of Christian Character* by Harvey Newcomb
One pastor has said, *"It should be read, studied, prayed over, and put into practice by parents, young ladies, and—yes—even young men! It should be in every home, and in the library of every young lady. It is a 'companion' book for a lifetime."* We could not agree more!

The Devotional Life of the Sunday School Teacher by J.R. Miller
Do not let the title fool you. This is an absolute must-read for every pastor and parent who has a concern about the eternal welfare of those under their care. Miller speaks directly to the heart of all who have been entrusted with the nurture of immortal souls. Although written nearly 100 years ago its message is as fresh as it was in the day it first came from the press.

Call us toll free at **1-877-666-9469**
E-mail us at **sgcb@charter.net**
Visit our web site at **solid-ground-books.com**

Printed in the United States
23230LVS00001B/382-396